This 'designerly loops' notebook belongs to:

_____
_____
_____
_____

Designerly Loops
By Linda N. Laursen and Louise M. Haase

1st Edition, 1st Print Run

© The Authors and Aalborg University Press, 2022

Graphic Design: Det Nye Sort
Printed by Toptryk Grafisk ApS, 2022
ISBN: 978-87-7210-758-5

Published by Aalborg University Press | forlag.aau.dk

The book is financially supported by Department of Architecture, Design & Media Technology, Aalborg University

PEER REVIEWED

All rights reserved. No part of this book may be reprinted or reproduced or utilized in any form or by any electronic, mechanical, or other means, now known or hereafter invented, including photocopying and recording, or in any information storage or retrieval system, without permission in writing from the publishers, except for reviews and short excerpts in scholarly publications.

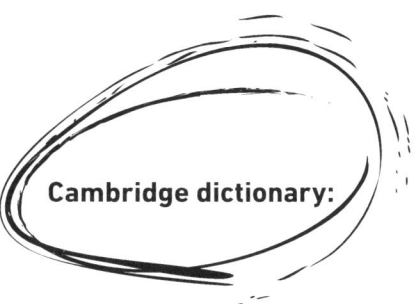

Cambridge dictionary:

to be in the loop:
'to be one of a group of people who have particular knowledge,
make important decisions or deal with
important situations'

a loop (in computing):
'a series of instructions that is repeated
until a particular thing happens'

a loop (in music):
'a short section of recorded music that is repeated
all through a song or part of a song'

TABLE OF CONTENTS

INTRO	**A DESIGNERLY EXPERTISE**	
	Welcome to a designerly notebook	12
	Designerly expertise	13
	The four designerly loops	17
	Promise and expectations	18
	Standing on the shoulders of: Design thinking and designerly research	20
	The notebook's structure	22
	How to read the book	24

LOOP I:	**IMMERSE**	**26**
	Immerse to move beyond assumptions	30
	Theory-in-brief	32
	Road Map Days 1–10	
	Day 1 Design Task and Arrangements	34
	Day 2 Boards 1.0	39
	Day 3 First Sketches	47
	Days 4–5 Context and Market Safari	50
	Theory in Brief	56
	Days 5–7 User Research	63
	Day 8 Product Sketching	67
	Day 9 Storyboard, Prep and Reflection	70
	Day 10 Milestone I	78
	Worksheets	
	WS#1 Prep and Plan	36
	WS#2 Persona Board 1.0	40
	WS#3 Context Board 1.0	42
	WS#4 Product Board 1.0	44
	WS#5 First Sketches	48
	WS#6 Context Safari – Context Board 2.0	52
	WS#7 Market Safari – Product Board 2.0	54
	WS#8 Interview Guide	60
	WS#9 User Research – Persona Board 2.0	64
	WS#10 Sketch on Specific Insights	68
	WS#11 Storyboard (Workarounds)	72

	Reflections	
	R#1 Modal Shifts	74
	R#2 To Move Beyond Assumptions	76

Page 7

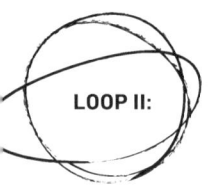

LOOP II:	PROBE	80

Proble into user's reasoning	85
Theory-in-brief	86

Road Map Days 11–20
- Day 11 Mock Up and Styleboard — 88
- Days 12-13 User Objections and Hooks — 97
- Day 14 Storyboard and Problem Focus — 103
- Days 15-16 Experiments — 106

Days 17-18-19 Low-fidelity Prototypes — 113
- Day 20 Milestone II — 120

Worksheets
- WS#12 Prep and Plan — 90
- WS#13 Mock Ups — 92
- WS#14 Style Board — 94
- WS#15 User Hooks and Objections — 98
- WS#16 Storyboard — 104
- WS#17 Feasibility Experiments — 108
- WS#18 Usability Experiments — 110
- WS#19 Problem setting — 114

Reflections
- R#3 Framing — 116
- R#4 Co-development of Problem and Solution — 118

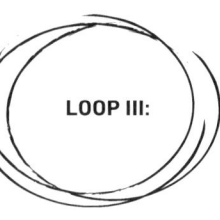

LOOP III:	PERSIST	116

Persists until all the dots are connected	126
Theory-in-brief	129

Road Map Days 21–30
- Day 21 Demands and Wishes — 131
- Days 22-23 Deconstruct and Define Elements and Structures — 137
- Days 24–30 Prototyping Day 5 Material — 141

Worksheets
- WS#20 Prep and Plan — 132
- WS#21 Demands and Wishes — 134
- WS#22 Product Disassembly Analysis — 138
- WS#23 Prototypes — 142

Reflections
- R#5 Solution-led Goal Analysis — 144
- R#6 Persists — 146

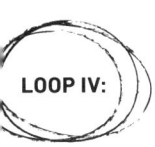

LOOP IV: **REFLECT** **148**

Reflect to storytell the position 153
Theory-in-brief 158

Road Map Days 31–40
    Days 31–32 Reflect on the Storyline and Position 154
    Days 33–39 Last round of Reflection, Storytelling and Prototyping 156

Reflections
    R#7 Modal Shifts 160
    R#8 Framing 162
    R#9 Co-development of Problem and Solution 164
    R#10 Dialogue with the Situation 166
    R#11 Solution-led Goal Analysis 168
    R#12 Reflective Practice 170

A DESIGNERLY EXPERTISE

'Reflective practice is a dialogue of thinking and doing through which I become more skilful'.

— Donald Schön

WELCOME TO A DESIGNERLY NOTEBOOK

If you want to build a designerly expertise, this book is for you. Because this book is all about 'doing' it. Of course, you may learn a lot from reading about the excessive number of design thinking methods and models that design researchers, design consultancies and practicing designers invented. But our studies of design experts revealed that in design, doing it is the key to building a designerly expertise.

In our latest research on design experts, we discovered, that you best acquire the skill and love of designing by jumping into the practice of designing. Therefore, we framed this book as 'a notebook'. Historically, notebooks have been spaces for designers for progressing their design while advancing their skills, thoughts and reasoning – a sort of space for collecting thoughts and reflections. We hope you will use this book as a regular moleskin. Draw in it, write in it, glue things into it. Use it as a place for design doing, note all your reflections, both those that emerge during your actions and those that arrive when you reflect on your actions.

When we started the research project on designerly expertise, and this book, our mission was to contribute with new research on: 'What design experts do?' collected in a format that is straightforward, relevant and at eye level for designers, students, other practitioners and businesses in general. We hope the book will help you when you are practising design to grasp what you do and have done. More importantly, we hope it will help you improve and understand how to build professional a designerly expertise.

DESIGNERLY EXPERTISE

In our research of extraordinary expert designers, we have had intense discussions on what 'designerly expertise' is and how we may best advance it at different levels. What do we already know? What can we see in practice that is not yet explained? And which pitfalls and shortcomings do people most often meet when trying to build a designerly expertise?

From previous research, we discovered that what designers focus on differs a lot depending on their level of expertise.[1] Therefore, in the theoretic framing of our research we build on the Dreyfus model of skill acquisition[2] (expertise). This shows that skill acquisition may be understood on levels from novices to experts (see Figure 1). One of the most important things to notice in the development from novice to expert is that, in the beginning, the ability to judge and prioritise is very low, whereas the dependency on rules (models, methods etc.) is very high. Experts, however, have intuitive grasps and visions of what to do and no dependency on rules. In fact, in our research, we found that most expert designers disregard models and methods.

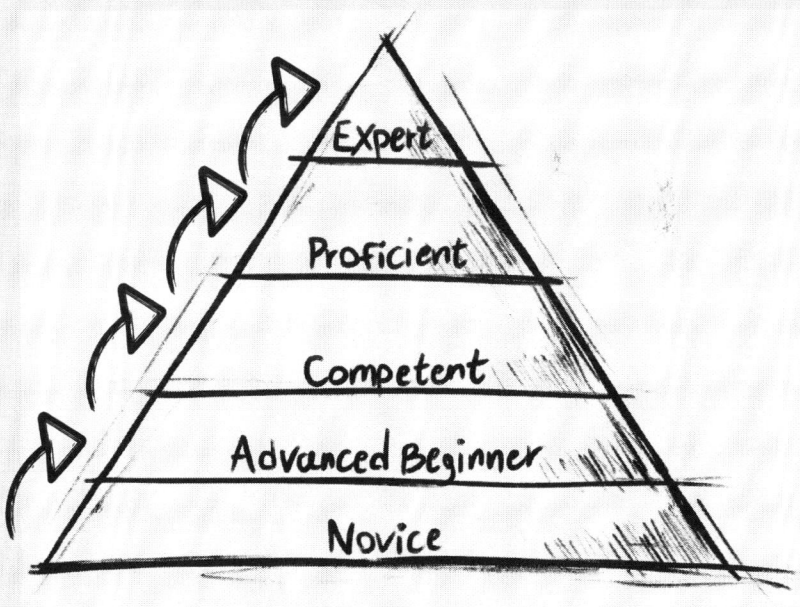

Figure 4. Building on Dreyfus and Dreyfus' skill acquisition model (1980)

---

1 Ericsson, K. A., Hoffman, R. R., & Kozbelt, A. eds. (2018). The Cambridge handbook of expertise and expert performance. Cambridge University Press.
2 Dreyfus, S. E., & Dreyfus, H. L. (1980). A five-stage model of the mental activities involved in directed skill acquisition (No. ORC-80-2). California University Berkeley Operations Research Center.

This aligns very well with the findings of our present research, where we also found that what occupies the minds of design experts varies a lot depending on whether we are talking about novices or competent designers. They think and do things differently. In other words, accumulating a design expertise is a matter of becoming good at judging, prioritising and having a vision of what to do. For that reason, design is often taught in a seemingly open, iterative, unstructured way. As novices have a high dependency on rules, methods, and models to develop skills of navigating and accumulating a sense of vision, they need a roadmap to learn navigation. Therefore, our research quest became to address this paradox.

THE RESEARCH QUESTION

Our research (and this book) therefore centers around not only understanding the approach of expert designers, but more specifically on what direction they move in at different 'stages' or parts of the design process. The ambition was to distill the essence of the design expertise approach, and conceptualise it into a model, which purpose was to train novices, providing them with key experiences to accumulate design expertise.

The questions that lead us in our research was therefore to understand: what directs expert designers at various stages of the design development? And how may such directions be conceptualized into a model for developing the skills of novices? Thus, the purpose of this book became to convey it in a manner, that actually supports and is approachable for novices.

THE RESEARCH DESIGN

The primary data for the research was collected through interviews with expert designers, and supported with secondary data (process presentations, sketches, videos, press, informal conversations etc.). The interviews were semi-structured to allow for both direction within the scope, but also to allow for flexibility to follow and understand unexpected avenues and findings.

"The question, then, is not whether we need to use the method of retrospective interview in the study of expertise, but, rather how best to use the method."[3]

In the following we will unveil how the research was conducted.
As preparation for the study, we first identified a number of expert designers. For that we deployed an information-oriented sampling strategy (Stake). As prior research uncovered, expert designers may be singled out as "highly creative or talented individuals" that are "successful and highly-regarded designers, with international reputations both within and beyond their professional peer groups."[4] We used a peer-to-peer recognition strategy, were we asked professionals in the design field, who they would point towards as outstanding or expert designers. This led us to 14 expert designers.

Second, these designers were contacted via email. As preparation, we informed them of the scope of the research: to understand the key elements of design performance or outstanding designers. Moreover, to get into depth with their approach and understand what guided them when designing, we asked each designer to identify one design project, which they were proud of. For this project, they were in advance asked to bring relevant materials on the design process, including notebooks, sketches, presentations, models, to not only support the occurrence of actions, but also to ensure a more in-depth and accurate recollection and reasoning. Our aim was to both unveil the process and the key tenets of the reasoning behind this particular design project.

---

3 Sosniak, L. A. (2006). Retrospective interviews in the study of expertise and expert performance. The Cambridge handbook of expertise and expert performance, 287-301.
4 Cross, N. (2004). Expertise in design: an overview. Design studies, 25(5), 427-441.

Previous studies show that the expert designer uses explicit problem decomposing strategies, which the novice appears to not possess. In order to identify these strategies, we collected data through semi-structured interviews, Each interview lasted 1 to 2 hours to allow for both a descriptive recollection of the design events and decomposing strategies, as well as a reflective discussion on the designer's reasoning.

All the interviews where subsequently transcribed and then coded based on the empirical findings using first the informants' own words that were then grouped into overall themes. The insights were then clustered according to different stages of the design process. Based on these, we found four key approaches applied by the expert designers across different stages in the design process, which will be briefly outlined in the following and laid out in detail in the rest of the book.

FINDINGS: FOUR DIRECTION LOOPS

In our interviews we found that expert designers' focus and expertise are built on four key approaches:

1. They immerse themselves in the challenges they work with to move beyond assumptions.
2. They continuously test prototypes and probe things with users to understand the users' reasoning.
3. They persist in redoing and remaking concepts until all the dots (or insights) from their research are connected.
4. They reflect to story tell about their design's positioning.

Each of these approaches hold a distinct direction that is matured before moving on to the next. In this book, we have sought to translate the expert designers' approaches to direction into a four loop model. We conceptualise them as loops, as we discovered that the experts' designers loops through the different approaches, until they have sufficiently matured their sense of direction.
Our hope is that we by outlining the loops can train you in this from the start of your design journey or your present experience level, so that you, too, may become an expert designer.

THE FOUR DESIGNERLY LOOPS

This notebook contains four design loops with suggested road maps, worksheets and reflection pages. We call these 'loops' to symbolise one of the most important things in designerly expertise, namely creating something based on your present knowledge and then reflecting on the results. Or, as Donald Schön terms this: reflection-in-action and reflection-on-action.[5] At the end of every loop, a new action is initiated; it is just more informed.

The loops are organised in a cyclic manner[6] with a structure and content that may drive reflection in and on your actions. We hope you will find these not only straightforward to follow, but that you will also (by the end of this book) realise these have been carefully laid out to stimulate deep design learning and to strengthen your designerly expertise.

We have tested the model that is conceptualised in this book on hundreds of people: You know who you are. Thank you! We even dare to promise you that by doing the worksheets, following the road map and noting theoretical reflections, you will, by the end of this book, have more insights into and experience in the core approaches to build a designerly expertise.

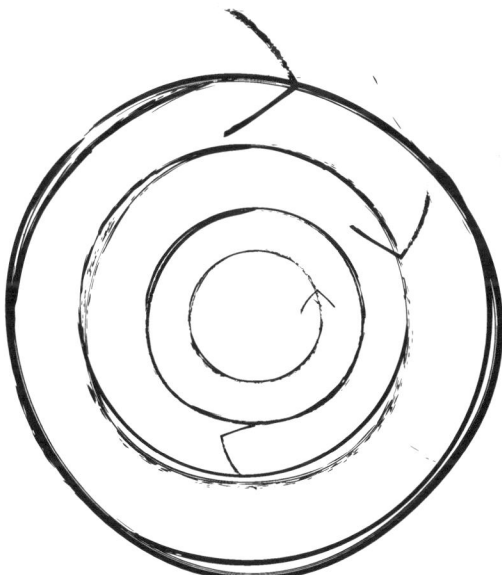

Figure 1. Four designerly loops

---

5 Schön, D. A. (1983). The reflective practitioner. Basic Books, New York.
6 Valkenburg, R., & Dorst, K. (1998). The reflective practice of design teams. Design studies, 19(3), 249–271.

PROMISE AND EXPECTATIONS

Our promise with this notebook is not to make a magic recipe that will produce a seminal design in 40 days. But we do promise to give you relevant experiences that will strengthen your knowledge, skills and competences so you develop into a highly competent designer. The only thing you need to do to achieve this is to promise us to act and reflect, work on the problem and the solution simultaneously, and focus on learning.

ACT AND REFLECT

You cannot sit still and think your way towards a great design. Nor can you sit in a team and discuss your way to a great design. We expect you to do design work. We will do our best to push you to take more action that will give you further experience, a further understanding of your intention, to ensure that you are progressing the project in the right direction. We believe you gain experience through experiences: hence, the name. But you only gain explicit insight from experiences if you remember to reflect. If you want to get the most out of your actions, you need to reflect on what you know and what you do not know to plan your next actions. We expect you to act – even if it feels like you are moving sideways or backwards – and we expect you to reflect on your actions – even when you think it is no use. If you start moving, you will soon figure out whether it is the right direction you are moving in. Otherwise, you just correct it along the way.

WORK ON THE PROBLEM AND THE SOLUTION SIMULTANEOUSLY

In practice, when you are in doubt, this book will probably not provide you with a clear answer, because every design problem is unique. Instead, we promise to help you either by suggesting critical actions or asking central questions. In design, the problem and solution emerge simultaneously, and part of figuring out what the problem actually is starts to create a possible solution.[7] These possible solutions may not turn out to be the final design, but you can use possible solutions for acquiring deeper learning about the problem.[8] Hence, if you cannot progress your understanding of the problem, start creating a possible solution. And when you cannot progress with the solutions, start going deeper into the problem situation.

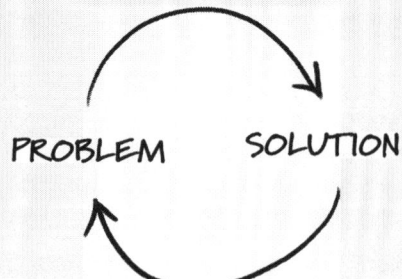

Figure 2. Problem-solution co-evolution

---

[7] Dorst, K., & Cross, N. (2001). Creativity in the design process: Co-evolution of problem–solution. Design Studies, 22 (5), 425– 437.

[8] Peirce, C. S. (1955). Philosophical writings of Peirce (Vol. 217). Courier Corporation.

FOCUS ON LEARNING

As for problems in the design process, we hope you run into them – better sooner than later. Some of our most rewarding lessons come from projects in difficult circumstances. We would be more worried if the process runs too smoothly, which is often a symptom of a very superficial understanding of the problem. If you follow the guidelines in this book, we will help you delve into your missing links and mistakes. Even if it feels uncomfortable, use these opportunities to take a step back from your project and look closely at its missing links and mistakes. Look at them through the eyes of the devil's advocate. These are key opportunities for learning and for improving your design.

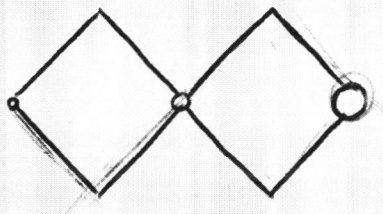

Figure 3. Design process expectations vs. reality

Sometimes, this also means failing – not just parts in the design process, but entire projects. All great designers have completely failed projects in their portfolio (though they may not often talk about them). However, failed projects are not just bad, even if it may feel like it. They give you an opportunity to reflect deeper and grow stronger competences.

When it is your turn to fail, promise us to forgive yourself, learn from it and get going again!

STANDING ON THE SHOULDERS OF:
DESIGN THINKING AND DESIGNERLY RESEARCH

In terms of theories, models and methods, we tried to combine the best of two worlds: namely, design thinking and designerly research. We see the design thinking concept is brilliant at making design accessible and making the value of design understandable. Similarly, we are fans of designerly theories, which without a doubt are central and important to explaining the design profession. One may also argue that many of them are not at eye level and do not offer any translation into how to learn or build your designerly expertise. Thus, one of the focuses of our work has been to combine the two.

DESIGN THINKING
One of the key qualities of design thinking that has inspired us is that it is easy to understand and approach. Typically, it portrays a four-to-seven-step iterative process model, with phases or steps that move from research/observations/emphasis to some kind of idea generation, prototyping and final design.[9] It is at eye level with newcomers to the design field. It is also easy to communicate and include adjacent professions. It is excellent at providing a starting point for any design journey. Unfortunately, it has shortcomings when it is implemented[10].

---

9 Brown, T. (2008). Design thinking. Harvard Business Review, 86 (6), 84.
10 Laursen, L. N., & Haase, L. M. (2019). The shortcomings of design thinking when compared to designerly thinking. The Design Journal, 22 (6), 813– 832.

DESIGNERLY RESEARCH

Similarly, we examined design research to anchor and build a theoretical foundation for this book. In a way, this book is built on the shoulders of giants, who have added substantially to our understanding of design expertise. Key parts of designerly research are often never implemented into design thinking material. This means that they become lost in translation. In many of the design thinking process models and methods used today, core parts of designerly expertise are omitted, forgotten or neglected, such as the situated-ness of design, the distinctive 'designerly ways of knowing' design and reflective practice. There might be several reasons for that, which we will not speculate on. The problem is that a significant contribution to our understanding of what constitutes design expertise is suddenly overlooked and never implemented. Our mission is to avoid this path and tie together the best parts of both design thinking and designerly research. In this book, we have identified the designerly research that is important to the journey of building designerly expertise and integrated it into an understandable and accessible framework.

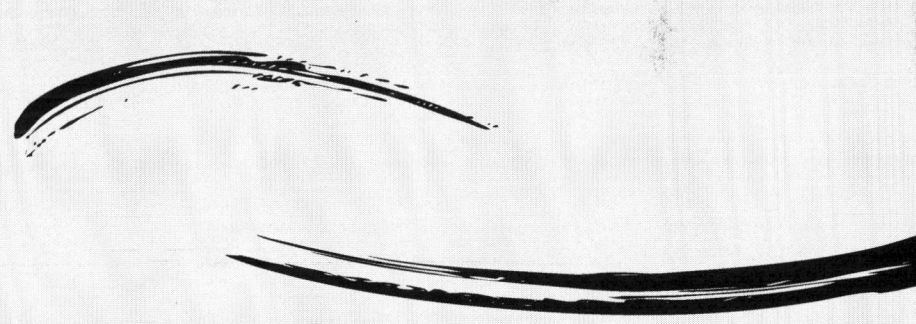

THE NOTEBOOK STRUCTURE

The book you are holding is built in a field of tension between our belief that one cannot put designerly expertise into a formula and the need to provide an apprenticeship road map for people who are new and need to navigate the practice and the theoretical landscape of design.
We want to provide not only a starting point but also a direction. We use the learnings from design thinking and design research, and our aspiration is to build the next generation of pragmatic designerly research and practice models. We try to highlight advice that is absolutely relevant and sort it out from the absolutely irrelevant.

APPRENTICESHIP
Design was initially taught as an apprenticeship in which the design master instructed the design apprentice in what to do. In this notebook, we provide a road map, worksheets, and theoretical reflection pages that together constitute such an apprenticeship approach. It may be like the first time you cook a dish. You followed a recipe, and someone guided and supported you step by step in what to do. Such structure and guidance are helpful if you are new to design and need to go through the process for the first time.
Our aspiration is to provide you with an apprenticeship experience. We will go through the steps in great detail day by day; this will provide you with essential instruction and guidance. But it will be as when you go on your first hike. It will be your own journey of discovery, an experience and learning no one can take away from you.

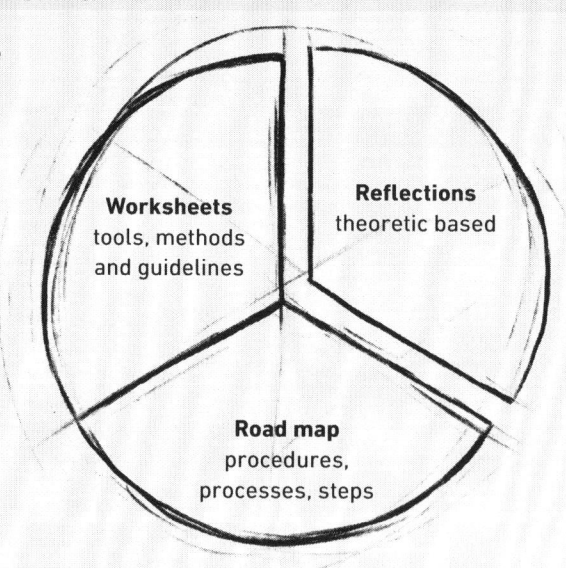

Figure 5. Road maps, worksheets and reflections

ROAD MAPS, WORKSHEETS AND REFLECTIONS
The typical pitfall of many process models is that they focus on the steps and confound the use of irrelevant iterations on the superficial level, with deep reflections that progress a design project and design skill. Because the reflection practice part is quite difficult and does not necessarily produce immediate results, it is absent from many product-oriented process models – unfortunately, because we argue, this is the core of what makes design practitioners move up the ladder of expertise.[11] By reframing, we hope to lay out a launching ramp to become a deeply reflective practitioner. Therefore, this book contains different road maps (sort of process recipes) and worksheets (sort of method selections), because they can meet people at eye level, to include and to give them a path through the aspects of design we consider most important. Thus, it builds on the strength of design thinking: how to provide a starting point and pave a path through a design. More importantly, we followed design actions with knowledge and learning (theoretical reflections), as a reflection in and on your actions, is core to becoming a competent practitioner.

---

11 Schön, D. (1938). The reflective practitioner. New York, p. 102.

HOW TO READ THE BOOK

This book is for you, whether you are about to embark on your first design adventure or you are an experienced professional in the design field. Anyone interested in design can read this book, but rather than just reading the book, we expect you to reflect on it too.

IF YOU ARE NEW TO DESIGN (NOVICE/ADVANCED BEGINNER)
... we advise you to follow road maps. Afterward, if you think you know better, feel free to create your own plan. But we have put much effort into laying them out and detailing them to help you become reflective, avoid typical pitfalls and arrive at situated prioritised design. Try to do the worksheets and reflection pages, even if you think some steps are redundant. Many of our students, for example, find it a bit unnecessary to create five or more prototypes for user testing because they think they already know what the best idea is. However, after being forced to do it, many of them are surprised that their understanding does not align with the users' or the users did not appreciate their preconception. Instead, they were taken by surprise by aspects and latent elements that were important. We do our very best to explain and support you through essential design actions; the essence of designerly expertise, so you novices and advanced beginners may 'do a design' and 'build an expertise'.

IF YOU ARE A DESIGN PROFESSIONAL (COMPETENT, PROFICIENT AND EXPERT)
. . . you may go through the book, do it, review it, find inspiration in it, configure it or reframe it. But try to be open and try out parts of the approach once. While we do not guarantee a seminal design, we guarantee deep, reflective learning. In situations where you have valuable experience and your intuition tells you to prioritise differently, feel free to follow your experience. We encourage you to situate and use the worksheets, road map and theoretical reflection pages in a meaningful manner. We think of it as how experienced chefs use recipes; they typically read recipes on a different level than the rest of us, picking up on renewing or interesting parts, experimenting to invent new recipes. But if they have never made or tasted a béarnaise sauce, even though they are professionals, they may try making it by the book once before rethinking it.

Loop 1

IMMERSE
TO MOVE BEYOND ASSUMPTIONS

'A practitioner's reflection can serve as a corrective to over-learning. Through reflection, he can surface and criticise the tacit understandings that have grown up around the repetitive experiences of a specialised practice and can make new sense of the situations of uncertainty or uniqueness which he may allow himself to experience'.

— Donald Schön

Notes

LOOP I **IMMERSE** • TO MOVE BEYOND ASSUMPTIONS

ROAD MAP

Road map 1*

Day 1 Design task and arrangements	Day 2 The first board	Day 3 The first Sketches	Day 4 Context and market safari + user research prep	Day 5 Context and market safari + user research prep
Day 6 User research	Day 7 User research	Day 8 Sketching on specific insights	Day 9 Storyboard, reflections and pitch prep	Day 10 Milestone I

*These are just suggestions. Remember to arrange and re-arrange the day after what works and makes sense to your team.

WORKSHEETS

- ☑ WS#1 Prep and Plan
- ☐ WS#2 Persona Board 1.0
- ☐ WS#3 Context Board 1.0
- ☐ WS#4 Product Board 1.0
- ☐ WS#5 First Sketches
- ☐ WS#6 Context Safari – Context Board 2.0
- ☐ WS#7 Market Safari – Product Board 2.0
- ☐ WS#8 Interview Guide
- ☐ WS#9 User Research – Persona Board 2.0
- ☐ WS#10 Sketch on Specific Insights
- ☐ WS#11 Storyboard (Workarounds)
- ☐ WS#12 Blind Spots

REFLECTION

- ☐ R#1 Modal Shifts
- ☐ R#2 To Move Beyond Assumptions

IMMERSE • TO MOVE BEYOND ASSUMPTIONS

APPROACH: In order to really decode a design situation, you need to move beyond obvious assumptions, blind spots and initial ideas. To do that, you first need to be aware of what you assume and what you do not know, and then puposefully move beyond your current perspective to widen your horizon beyond present ignorance.

In this work package, we provide the road map, worksheets and reflections that will help you to move beyond the obvious: your current understanding, immediate assumptions, primary ideas and blind spots. The first work package in this book will help you to make sure that, during the foundation, you move further to integrate different perspectives and move between modes – a sort of modal shift.[12] Complete this work package when you are starting a new product, category or domain, and you need to ensure that you understand the design situation far beyond the obvious.

ASSUMPTIONS

You, we (and everyone else we meet) have standard assumptions, norms we ascribe to product categories. These beliefs about the users, the situation and the context keep on shadowing our sight. But if these are captured, made explicit, said aloud and placed on the wall, we can get them out of our heads, understand them, evaluate them, put a perspective on them and develop them further – make sense of them. They will not keep on standing in the way; instead, observation and knowledge will crystallise into insights that frame a perception of the design situation. This is the first sense-making step in designing.[13]

---

[12] Cross, N. (2006). Design as a discipline. Designerly Ways of Knowing, pp. 95–103.
[13] Kolko, J. (2010). Abductive thinking and sensemaking: The drivers of design synthesis. Design Issues, 26 (1), 15–28.

KILL YOUR DARLINGS
In design, we often say: 'Kill you darlings' – your first ideas – that you tend to grow very fond of. We will not kill your darlings. We will simply help you reflect on them and move beyond them. Maybe deeper, maybe further, maybe in a different direction. Our experience is that if you start with a standard understanding of the design situation, you will get a standard design. Design is like magic; once you learn the trade, it is pretty straightforward, rational and realistic. The first step in making an extraordinary and meaningful design is to go beyond the ordinary and the meaningless and search for the bits and pieces, insights no one has made sense of before, to make a great foundation.

The road map provides an overview of our activities. We have laid them out in days to ease the planning. Time boxing gives an impression of the relative extent (time, effort) that we recommend you spend on activities. The worksheets and reflections help you start doing and reflecting. Even though you have never tried using them before, just try. Remember: 'A journey of a thousand miles begins with a single step'.

THEORY IN BRIEF

This first loop, immersing oneself beyond the obvious, is based on design research that concerns novelty or, rather, the lack of novelty in designers' work. In a protocol study of nine experienced industrial designers, Kees Dorst and Nigel Cross found that, when the nine designers were presented with the exact same design situation, brief, assignment and information, they in fact arrived at the same conceptual design solution.

> 'All nine designers got this idea, and all of them reported upon it as an original idea, a key concept in their solution. The majority end up with the same conceptual design solution'.[14]

Thus, the aim of this loop, which is omitted from many design books, is to go beyond the same obvious insights, such as biases and guesses, to widen your perspective of the design situation – to pursue inexplicit, rare and atypical insights that are novel and significant. To look beyond the immediate design sitation - seeing, recognising and turning such information into insights requires deliberate training. Such research will only lead to creative concepts with a skilled designer's interpretation. That means their choice of what is particularly relevant in the current design situation.[15]

For example, for our research, we interviewed Frank Stephenson, who designed the Mini Cooper (as well as the Fiat 500 and many other extraordinary cars). We found that what distinguished him from the 14 other car designers (whose redesign for the Mini was not chosen) was his deep immersion beyond the obvious. We found his search for novel, deep and surprising information striking and the differentiating factor between him and the 14 other designers, who all got a month to design the car and five months to model it up in full scale. Of those months, Frank spent 80% of his time 'immersing beyond the obvious' and only 20% drawing (and in fact, only 5% of the time drawing the design of the final car). Frank also describes his process as different from the other designers' processes:

> I was curious to see what they were inspired by, how they got the ideas for their designs; for me, it was interesting. Because they all looked different, and I was shocked, because nobody did what I did, which was for me the only way I could design a car with as characteristic or strong a personality as the Mini.
>
> What I did was ... because the Mini was the same car from 1959 to 1999, forty years, I thought about what if it had changed every 10 years. 1969, 1979, 1989 – what would be that look for every decade. So, the first week I used to research and design the 1969 Mini, instead of going straight to the final design'.[16]

---

14 Dorst, K., & Cross, N. (2001). Creativity in the design process: Co-evolution of problem–solution. Design Studies, 22 (5), 433.
15 Kolko, J. (2010). Abductive thinking and sensemaking: The drivers of design synthesis. Design Issues, 26 (1), 15– 28.
16 Laursen (2018) Dta from an interview with Frank Stephenson.

Frank's design was chosen unanimously. His expertise is characterised by the way he shaped the design situation, by finding and identifying new perspectives and information to be considered. He looked for information about how times had changed and, with them, the cars, for example how people in the 1970s were into safety, drove longer, were taller etc. Therefore, he drew a 1970s version of the Mini with big welding, a higher cabinet, larger truck etc. He spent time researching and designing the car decade through decade, as an evolution through time. He reframed the task as a naturally evolutionary task and sought information on the evolution of cars.

Defining a problem is recognised by Donald Schön as a central element to design expertise:

> To formulate a design problem to be solved, the designer must frame a problematic design situation: set its boundaries, select particular things and relations for attention, and impose on the situation a coherence that guides subsequent moves.[17]

By pushing for deep, diverse and conflicting information, he pushed for a field of tension for his problem and solution to co-emerge in, an intuitive reframing of the problem. Reframing allows for the rephrasing of the problem or the situation, which is thereby extended beyond the obvious to determine whether the problem is actually a symptom of another problem and, eventually, to identify the core of both the problem and the solution.[18] A designer's push and pursuit for diverse and conflicting information, perspectives and ideas is, in fact, one of the key elements that characterises design expertise.[19]

---

17 Schön, D. (1938). The reflective practitioner, New York, p. 102.
18 Dorst, K. (2011). The core of 'design thinking' and its application. Design Studies, 32 (6), 521–532.
19 Cross, N. (2004). Expertise in design: An overview. Design Studies, 25 (5), 427–441.
    Lawson, B. (2006). How designers think: The design process demystified. Routledge.
    Buchanan, R. (1992). Wicked problems in design thinking. Design Issues, 8 (2), 5–21.

DAY 1
DESIGN TASK AND ARRANGEMENTS

INSTRUCTIONS
- Kickoff: Settling or getting the brief. The brief defines the type of product and the user group, e.g. *you have to design a lamp for a painter.*
- Video a: Designerly direction
- Video b: Immerse yourself to move beyond one's assumptions

TEAMWORK

Aim
Familiarise yourself with your team, the task and Loop I material.

Process

☐ **Read Loop 1**
(including the introduction, theory, road map I, boards and reflections.) While reading, note what needs to be arranged and practicalities (e.g. contact users and plan, remember long days, bring cameras etc.). Individually note questions and problems during this loop. WS #1

Share insights from reading Loop 1.
☐ Write a collective mind map of arrangements, practicalities, questions and problems in Loop 1.
☐ Help each other with taking tasks on this list. Individuals volunteer to take a to-do task and help each other find solutions to challenges. Brainstorm, write on sticky notes, and agree on a preliminary answer/solution that will help you move forward.

Agree on the boundaries for teamwork:
☐ Please also review personal aspirations, ambitions, investments, efforts and practicalities.

TEAMWORK

Aim
Find three users willing to partake in your user research.

Process

- [ ] Research online where representatives of your user groups are near you. Strategically select whom to collaborate with. (Diversity is preferred, for example a fitness yoga instructor, a trained yogi and Buddhist yoga. Look for demographic differences such as age/gender/types.)
- [ ] Contact the users, and arrange visits and interviews with them. (Remember not to bother or make the involvement too extensive for them; it is just a visit with a short interview.) Perhaps you could use social media, for example make an Instagram story or Facebook post asking for contacts.

NOTE: Meet your users when they are available, if not during the day, then during the evening or nights.

WORKSHEET

WS#1 • PREP AND PLAN

Start here by noting tasks, aspects and considerations that come to mind while going through the road map, worksheets and reflection of Loop 1.

Designed by: _____   Date: _____   Iteration #: _____

User research arrangement:
Who, how, where, what?

Linda Nhu Laursen and Louise Møller Haase (2022) Designerly Loops.

Ideas/opportunities:
Note anything that comes to your mind contacts/resources/etc

Materials list:
What do we need

Challenges/obstacles:
Note anything that comes to your mind

Other:
Issues to remember or you came to think of

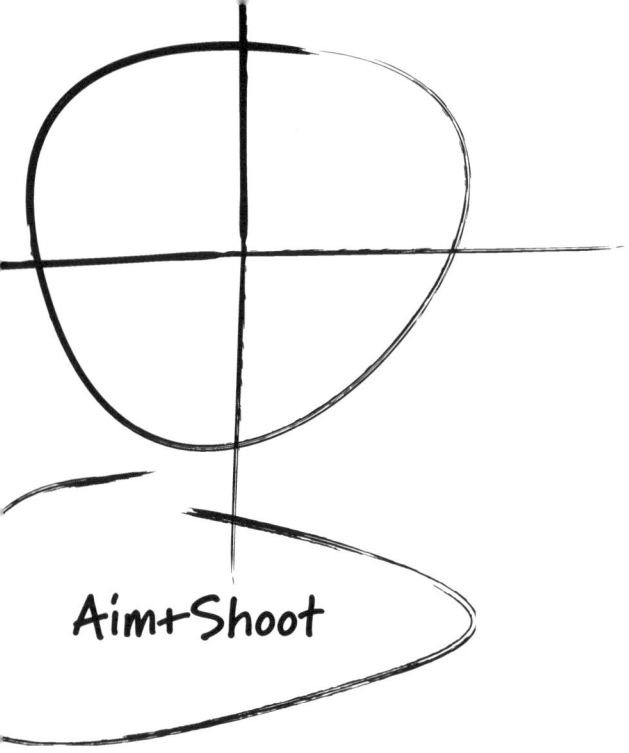

DAY 2
THE FIRST BOARDS

INSTRUCTIONS | Video 1: Boards: Personas, Context, Product Board

TEAMWORK

Aim
- Development of Persona Board (WS#2), Context Board (WS#3) and Product Board (WS#4)

Process
- The team subdivides into smaller groups of two to three people. Each group meets and develops a first version of each board, respectively, a Persona Board (WS#1), Context Board (WS#2) and Product Board (WS#3), based on desk research. The first version of the boards is based on desk research and the teams' current understanding. It helps the teams to make their starting point and hypothesis explicit, so they can later progress from them.

TEAM DISCUSSION

Aim
- Discussion to develop hypothesis and questions from boards.

Process
- Each of the smaller groups presents their boards to the others. Reflect on your boards so it becomes apparent what you know or do not know (about the user, context, and product), and what it is important you get answers to or you are curious about during the following days.
- Discuss what you actually know and what you have guessed or assumed, as well as any prejudices you might have concerning the user, context and product. The conclusions from your discussion are noted as hypotheses and questions (e.g. *hypothesis: Painters need to see all the nuances on the surface of the wall. Hypothesis: Yoga instructors like ancient Asian aesthetic references or questions: How many tools does the painter usually bring? When are they involved in the process? Who do they interface with?*) on collective personas, product and context boards pinned on the wall.

WORKSHEET

WS#2 PERSONAS BOARD 1.0

You work through a personas board to deepen your understanding of the specific target group (e.g. for painters – professionals, hobby artists, landscape painters).
Print photos, and pin them on this page.

Designed by: _____ Date: _____ Iteration #: _____

Feeling

Psychographics

Identity →

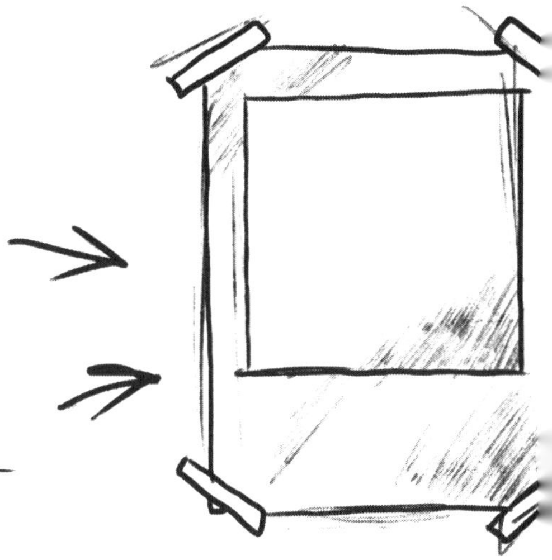

Type of color

Type of personal items

Linda Nhu Laursen and Louise Møller Haase (2022) Designerly Loops.

Place characteristic
photo here

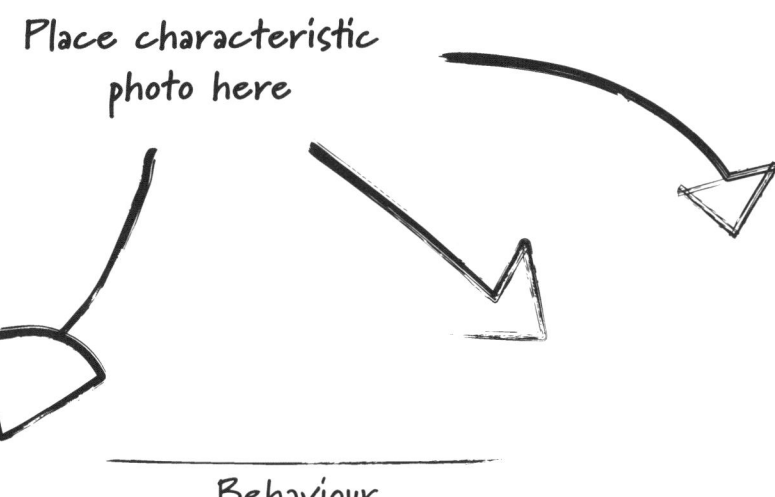

_____
Behaviour

Facts

_____
Demograph

_____
Geography

WORKSHEET

WS#3 CONTEXT BOARD 1.0

You work through a context board to deepen your understanding of the specific context (e.g. a construction site, private home, outdoor, indoor). *Print photos, and pin them on this page.*

Designed by: _____   Date: _____   Iteration #: _____

Contex

Place photo of things/ stuff/ tools

Linda Nhu Laursen and Louise Møller Haase (2022) Designerly Loops.

Board

Place photo of
Environment on
a great day
+
BAD DAY

WORKSHEET

WS#4 PRODUCT BOARD 1.0

You work through a context board to deepen your understanding of the type of product and the current market (e.g. a lamp: Is it standing, mobile, wearable?). Remember, you need to regroup to make dimensions and categories that make sense.

Designed by: _____   Date: _____   Iteration #: _____

SMALL ―――――――――――――――――――――

Linda Nhu Laursen and Louise Møller Haase (2022) Designerly Loops.

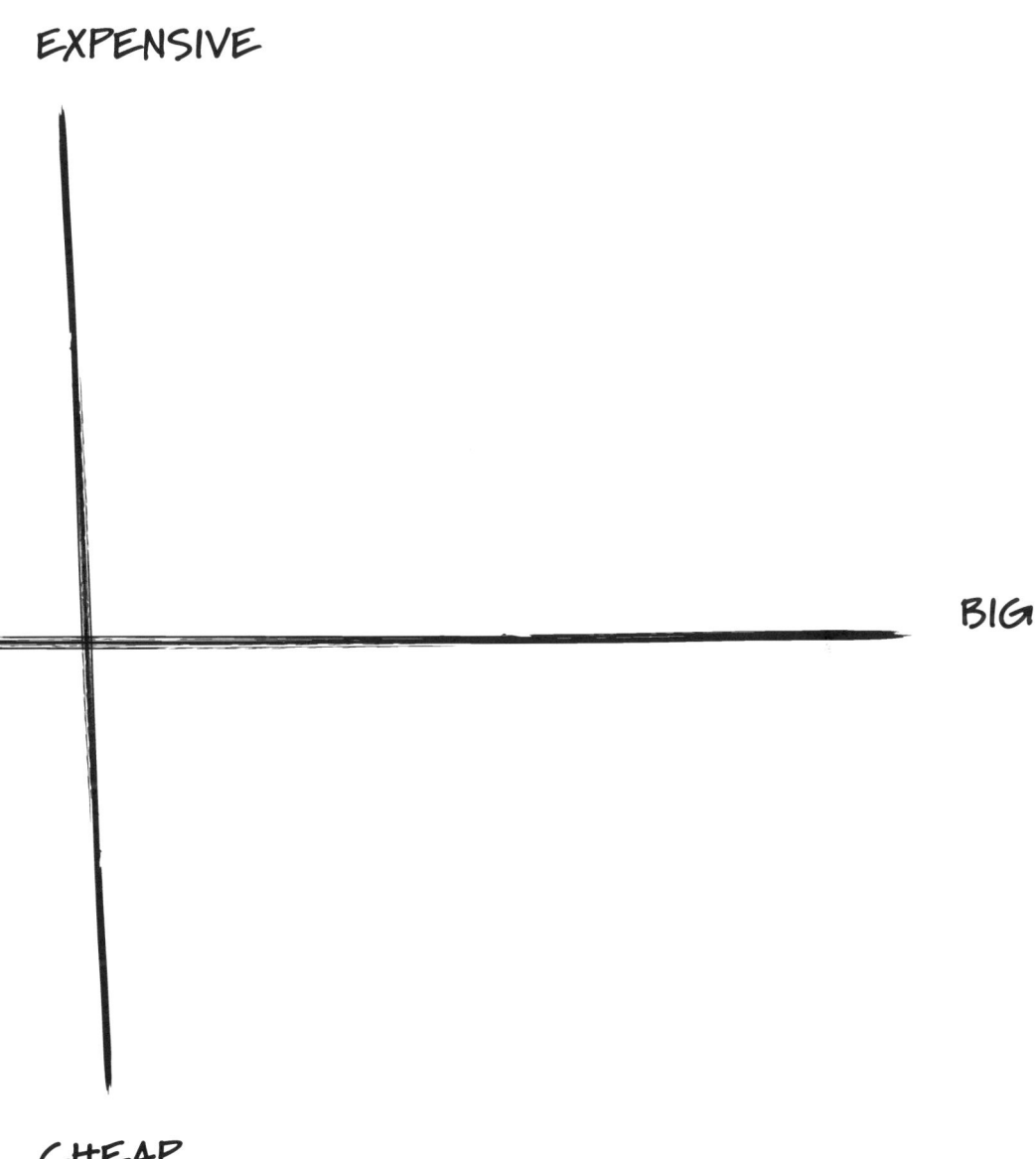

Sketching process

- Pen thickness
- Paper size
- Time/phase

Generate Ideate Refine

LOOP I IMMERSE • TO MOVE BEYOND ASSUMPTIONS

DAY 3
THE FIRST SKETCHES

INSTRUCTIONS Video 2: Sketch

TEAMWORK

Aim
Collect your first thoughts and ideas about the project.

Process
- [ ] Each person develops a minimum of three ideas that are sketched on the following page. You are welcome to use inspiration from your hypothesis boards.

TEAM DISCUSSION

Aim
Share, qualify and develop individual ideas

Process
- [ ] Each person shares ideas, and you each note and discuss why you think it may work or may not work about personas, context and the product or market.
- [ ] Afterwards, five to seven ideas are selected for further development. Then each person is assigned one of the selected ideas, which is not their own, and further develops it.
- [ ] Before the day is over, the ideas should be sketched and pinned up on the walls.

Questions, doubts and assumptions about the user, context and market are also noted for the next day's research.

WORKSHEET

WS#5 FIRST SKETCHES

Develop a minimum of three ideas that are sketched on the following page. You are welcome to use inspiration from your hypothesis boards.

Designed by: _____   Date: _____   Iteration #: _____

Sketch an idea for a product here ↘

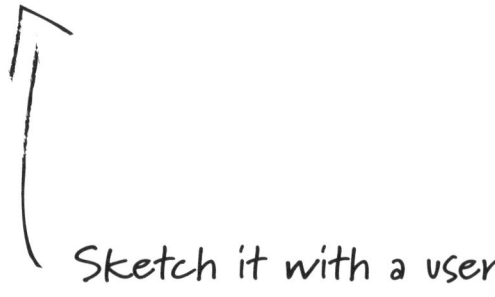

Sketch it with a user

Linda Nhu Laursen and Louise Møller Haase (2022) Designerly Loops.

Sketch a second product idea here

Sketch another idea here

DAY 4 + 5

CONTEXT AND MARKET SAFARI + USER RESEARCH PREP

INSTRUCTIONS | Video x: Context and Market Safari

TEAMWORK

Aim
Research the context of your users and the market of the products

Process
- [ ] Use half an hour to find places or environments that can help you understand the context of your user and the markets of the products *(e.g. if your user paints buildings, you could visit a construction site (preferably places other than where you plan on doing user research later in the week) and a professional painting shop.*
- [ ] Go on a context safari in smaller groups, and visit the different environments and contexts. Bring a camera, and remember to document. You could, for example, participate in yoga classes and make field notes. (How does it feel as a newcomer?) Especially keep an eye out for surprises, things that puzzle you or items different from your expectations.

TEAM DISCUSSION

Aim
Gather the insights from your safaris on a context board 2.0 (WS#6) and product board 2.0 (WS#7).

Process:
- [ ] Each minor group presents their experiences through photos.
- [ ] Look at your context board and product board. What did you learn? Were your assumptions and understanding confirmed, or did your understanding change? Your deeper and key insights should then be arranged on a context board and a product board (think about how your initial were confirmed, rejected, deepened or what surpriced you).
- [ ] Compare your photos from the safari, and develop new and deeper boards 2.0: Look at where they are most different. Where were you mistaken? What surprised you the most? What aspects are just odd ones out? Questions to the users are also noted.

USER RESEARCH PREP

INSTRUCTIONS Video y: User research

TEAMWORK

Aim
Develop an interview guide ((see page 50-53; Theory in brief guides for context and user research).

Process
- [ ] Brainstorm all the questions that could be relevant to ask your users. Write down everything without filtering first. Then cluster and categorise. Think about what you really want to know about your users (consider both functional, emotional and social needs).
- [ ] Check your boards. How will you get answers to your hypothesis or things you are curious about?

WORKSHEET

WS#6 CONTEXT BOARD 2.0 – FROM SAFARI

Take photos of environments, details, tools and aspects that are surprising to you during your context safari. Take rich photos that you think capture key aspects. Then work through your context board again to capture and deepen your understanding of the specific context (e.g. a construction site, private homes, outdoors, indoors).

Designed by: _____   Date: _____   Iteration #: _____

Details ↘

Central Parts

Linda Nhu Laursen and Louise Møller Haase (2022) Designerly Loops.

Enviroment

Unexpected things

Tools/ Things

WORKSHEET

WS#7 PRODUCT BOARD 2.0 – FROM MARKET SAFARI

Take photos of environments, details, tools and aspects that are surprising to you during your market safari. Take rich photos that you think capture key aspects. You work through a product board to capture your deepened understanding of the type of product and the current market (e.g. a lamp—standing, mobile, wearable).

Designed by: _____   Date: _____   Iteration #: _____

Shelf in the store

Highend product

Specific style

Cheap product

THEORY IN BRIEF GUIDES FOR CONTEXT AND USER RESEARCH

For designers, it is essential to understand the users, the context and the market they are designing for, which provides valuable insights into the design process. Moreover, context and user research are tools in the design toolbox that need to be mastered.

UNDERSTANDING USERS

The aim of user and context research is to understand the users' needs, values, wishes and dreams and to create a design that fulfils these. Or as Buxton[20] explains it: '. . . to really succeed, (. . .) products must be reconciled to the needs and values of the individuals, . . . societies, and cultures to which they are being targeted'. It is therefore important that user and context research not only disclose functional needs, but also socioemotional needs[21]. For instance, if the product is a car, the functional need for most people may be to get from A to B. However, there may also be some emotional needs to fulfil, for instance, to feel safe or comfortable. And finally, there might also be some social needs, for instance: 'looking smart while driving'. Below is an overview of the different types of needs in the figure.

Functional needs: Non-emotional needs the products should fulfil
Emotional needs: How you want to feel while you use the product
Social needs: How you want to be perceived when you use the product

Figure 6. Types of needs

---

20 Bill Buxton (2007). Sketching user experiences: Getting the design right and the right design. Morgan Kaufmann Publishers: San Francisco.
21 Ulwick, A. (2005). What customers want: Using outcome-driven innovation to create breakthrough products and services. McGraw-Hill: New York.

SAY-DO-MAKE
User research may be conducted in many ways. Some do interviews, observations or user tests. Others engage in long-term field studies or arrange workshops with users. It all depends on what they are looking for. Sanders[22] argues that, if we focus on what users say, we get access to what they say and think and, therefore, the need they know they have. If we focus on what they do, we get access to what they do and how they do it and, thus, insights into needs that they could not articulate. This may include insights into what they feel or what they wish or dream. Finally, if we ask users to co-create a solution with us, we can see how they make sense of things. This provides insights into needs and desires they are not aware of.

Focus	What user SAYS	What user DOES	What user MAKES
Insight	What they think and say	What they do and how they do it	How they conduct sense making
Needs	They know	They have not been able to articulate, including wishes and dreams	Needs and desires they are not aware of

Figure 7. Say-do-make

---

22 Sanders & Strappers (2012). Convivial toolbox: Generative research for the front end of design, BIS publishing, Amsterdam.

FIVE USER RESEARCH METHODS

It is vital to plan user interviews. When planning, it is important to consider what level of user information is needed for the project. Is it enough to have insights into the needs that the user knows, or is it also important to have insights into the needs that the user cannot articulate or is not even aware of? Sperschneider and Bagger[23] formulated five user research methods that give access to both what the users SAY and what they DO:[24]

1 **Situated interview – tell me what you do**
Qualitative interview with the user in the place or situation where the user will utilise the future product. An interview guide is made and brought along; however, the interview should be more than a conversation, where all the questions are touched upon during the conversation. New questions may also derive from the conversation, and these also are asked.

2 **Simulated use – show me how I should do it**
The user is asked to simulate how they do things today, for instance, a workflow or daily routines. If it is not possible for the user to show this in the actual situation, where they can act it out (see No. 3), set up a laboratory where they can simulate the use. Meanwhile, the user is asked to explain what they do. The users are supported by questions such as: Why do you do this? Or why is this important?

3 **Acting out – show me your normal procedure**
The user is asked to act out their normal procedures or workflow in the actual setting. Meanwhile, the user is asked to explain what they do. The users are supported by questions such as: Why do you do this? Or why is this important?

4 **Shadowing – let me walk with you**
The designer follows the user in their daily routine and observes what they do, for example for a day. The designer may have developed some questions or some hypothesis they want answers to. But for the most part, the designer observes in silence and looks for things that are interesting or surprising.

5 **Apprenticeship – teach me how**
The designer places himself or herself in the role of the user by becoming an apprentice of the user. The designer learns about daily routines, how they should do things and engage as if they are a colleague, a collaborator, a friend or whatever the situation asks for. Having tried out different tasks, the designer can formulate and reformulate questions about the things they want to know.

---

23 Sperschneider, W., & Bagger, K. (2003). Ethnographic fieldwork under industrial constraints: Toward design-in-context. International Journal of Human-Computer Interaction, 15(1), 41-50.
24 Sanders & Strappers (2012). Convivial toolbox: Generative research for the front end of design, BIS publishing, Amsterdam.

PRACTICAL ADVICE
One of the keys to good context and user research is that you go there. It is not enough to do it on your desktop. To really gain precise and usable insights into a context, you must go there yourself. As an user-research expert Anna Kirah says, *'Don't go to the zoo. Go to the jungle!'*. Likewise, you cannot get a precise understanding of the users you are designing for by using yourself or anyone you know as a reference. You must talk to real users, preferably in the physical surroundings where they will use the product. Some market research can be conducted online; however, we highly recommend that it be supplemented with a visit to retail stores or other places where you can buy the product.

BE KIND
Another key to collecting high-quality context and user research is to consider how you can make the user comfortable during the research. It can be hard to be interviewed or observed for a whole day. For some, it may feel like being placed on display. So if this is going to work, you have to build a space for a nice conversation.
Moreover, be careful not to judge. The moment you do this, the user is likely to stop sharing the type of insights you need and provide superficial answers. Please be open, kind and curious.
Regarding observations, pay attention to what the users does and what they are focusing their attention on. Look for things they do that they are not aware of and ask them kindly why they do this. People tend to develop workarounds if products are not working properly or if they cannot understand them. If you identify a workaround, be curious about why it was created in the first place – and note it.

WS#8 INTERVIEW GUIDE

Brainstorm all the questions that could be relevant to ask your users.
Think about what you really want to know about your users.
Consider questions related to functional, emotional and social needs.
Write down everything without filtering first. Then cluster and categorise.

Designed by: _____   Date: _____   Iteration #: _____

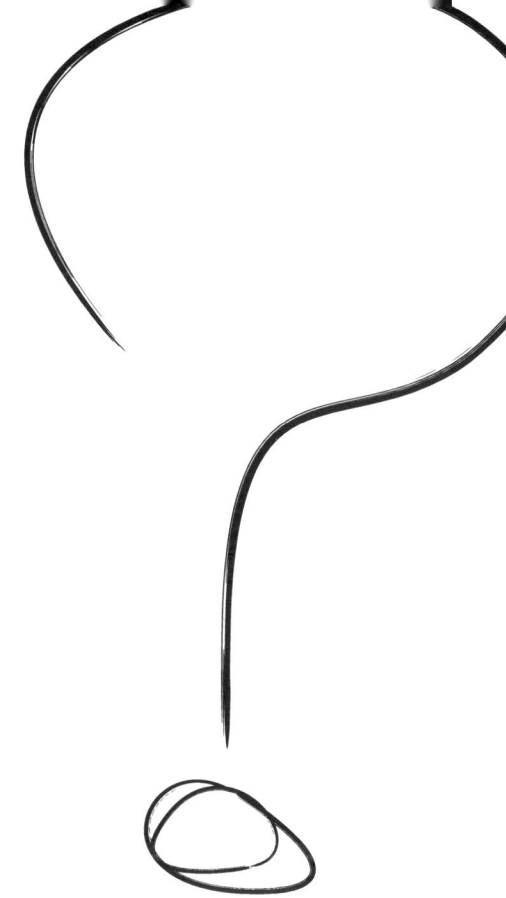

SKETCH:

LOOP 1 IMMERSE • TO MOVE BEYOND ASSUMPTIONS

DAY 5+6+7
USER RESEARCH

TEAMWORK

(Plan the days so they fit your users.)

Aim: Interview different users

Process:
- [ ] Divide into smaller groups of two to three people to go on different interviews. Agree beforehand on your roles in the interview. For example, one asks questions from the interview guide. The other listens really carefully and asks follow-up questions and looks for surprises, workarounds or any other odd things that may reveal hidden insights. (Additional questions on adjacent topics will preferably go at the end of the interview.) Yet another will document with photos, videos, taperecording and notes.
- [ ] Do the interviews.
- [ ] Make agreements to show/test your prototypes on days 16–17

Especially keep an eye out for surprises, things that puzzle you or are different from your expectations.

After the user interviews

TEAMWORK

Aim: The most important insights from each interview should be collected on Personas Board 2.0 (WS#8) with concrete observations, quotes and themes.

Process:
- [ ] The group is divided into smaller groups of two to three people. Each subgroup goes through the recording of their interviews and transcripts of key quotes and topics. Then, work on a redo and deepening of the previously made personas board, based on your user research and the insights you identified. Insights are the observations that you choose to advance in your design process.
- [ ] What surprised you? What did you confirm? What will you reject? What do we know more about? Collect all of your new knowledge and insights on a Personas Board 2.0.
- [ ] Compare your Board 1.0 with the new Personas Board 2.0: Where do they differ the most? Where were you most mistaken? What were you most surprised about?

WORKSHEET

WS#9 PERSONAS BOARD 2.0

Take photos and collect quotes that are surprising to you during your user research. Take rich photos that you think capture key aspects. Then work through your personas board to capture your deepened understanding of *the specific target group (e.g. for painters, professional, hobby artists, landscape painters)*.

Designed by: _____   Date: _____   Iteration #: _____

" Surprising quote

" Interesting quo

Photo of something surprising

Linda Nhu Laursen and Louise Møller Haase (2022) Designerly Loops.

Photo of something
they treasure

" Charachteristic quote

Place a photo of a
great detail

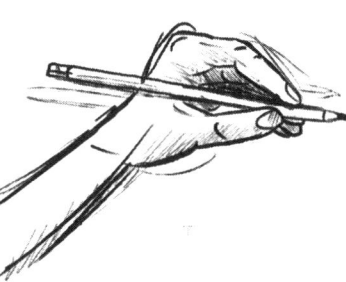

SKETCH

DAY 8
SKETCH ON SPECIFIC INSIGHTS

INSTRUCTION | Rewatch Video 2: Sketch

INDIVIDUAL WORK

Aim
Every team member develops three design solutions for parts of the problem, based on the research and boards, Version 2.0.

Process
☐ Individual idea development: Select a specific insight from the user research or market content safari, and develop an idea that only considers this. Draw it up, or make small cardboard models, for example one design for a lamp that is easy to transport, another design that provides the perfect reading light, or another design that fits perfectly on the market as the only cheap, one-time-use lamp.

After the user interviews

TEAMWORK

Aim
Build the different partial solutions together

Process:
☐ Joint idea development: Each team member presents solutions to different insights, and the group works on integrating selected ones into more complete concepts.
☐ In the end, six concepts are developed and selected to be redrawn with markers.

WORKSHEET

WS#10 SKETCH ON SPECIFIC INSIGHTS

Write a long list of insights (problems, workarounds, opportunities, priorities),
for example:
- The painter needs a lamp that is easy to carry.
- The painter needs a lamp that is sturdy if it is dropped.
- The lamp needs to provide diffused light.

Designed by: _____ Date: _____ Iteration #: _____

Insights:

Insights:

Linda Nhu Laursen and Louise Møller Haase (2022) Designerly Loops.

Insights: _____

Insights: _____

Insights: _____

DAY 9
STORYBOARD, REFLECTION AND PITCH PREP

INSTRUCTION | Video 3: **Storyboard** (and boards do-over)

INDIVIDUAL WORK

Aim
Every team member develops a storyboard.

Process
- [ ] Individual development of a storyboard. WS #11 Think about where you start the story. What is the scene? What are the key pain points, workarounds, irritations? What works well?

TEAMWORK

Aim
Build a joint storyboard

Process
- [ ] Share your individual storyboards. Discuss differences. Why are they different? How can we argue about what to focus on?
- [ ] Develop an integrated storyboard.

Sketch:

INDIVIDUAL WORK

Aim
Reflection on Loop 1.

Process
- ☐ Find your boards, versions 1.0 to 2.0 (that contain your own photos). Note the key differences.
- ☐ Find your first and second round of sketches. Note the key distinctions.
- ☐ Do reflection #1 Modal Shifts + reflection #2 Beyond Assumptions.

TEAMWORK

Aim
Make a design pitch for Milestone I that collects all your insights on your design in a story.

Process
- ☐ Share your reflections in the group. Discuss and collect them into a joint reflection, with particular focus on the key leaps of understanding in the various boards 1.0 and 2.0, respectively, as well as the first and second rounds of sketching.
- ☐ Connect all these into the first part of the presentation, which explains what you learned that you did not know 10 days ago, and how your design has progressed accordingly.
- ☐ Gather your storyboard, eight concepts, plus your leaps in the process into a design pitch.

WS#11 STORYBOARD

Think about where you are starting the story. What is the scene? Think about the situation (e.g. does a professional painter need a lamp? For what? Why? When? What does the situation look like?). How does the situation unfold? (What are key pain points, workarounds, irritations? What works well?). Use the storyboard to identify what to focus on.

Storyboards have different purposes in different parts of the design progression. In these first storyboards, the aim is to map situations, problems, atmospheres, feelings, and contexts. At this stage make sure to, include a lot of details, both factual and symbolic.[25] It is an analytical tool to understand contexts. It is about positioning the product in the life and context of a user.

Designed by: _____ Date: _____ Iteration #: _____

1	2
3	4

---

25 Roozenburg, N. F., & Eekels, J. (1995). Product design: Fundamentals and methods.

5 _____

6 _____

7 _____

8 _____

9 _____

10 _____

REFLECTION #1

MODALSHIFTS[26]

Designerly thinkers rapidly switch their attention between tasks and types of activities.[27] For instance, they might focus on the overall project and then on a smaller detail of the project, or they might rapidly shift between analysis, synthesis and evaluation. This modal shift has been found to heighten the quality of the eventual solution.[28]

On the following pages, please reflect on your modal shifts. First, draw a timeline and, then, as a mini thumbnail note, key activities. Then, with a coloured pen, write the task, type of activity and the perspective (user, context or market, whole products or detail of parts, analysis or synthesis etc.).

26 Laursen & Haase (2019). The shortcomings of design thinking when compared to designerly thinking, The Design Journal
27 Akin, Ö., & Lin, C. (1995). Design protocol data and novel design decisions. Design Studies, 16(2), 211–236.
28 Cross, N. (2006). Design as a discipline. Designerly Ways of Knowing, pp. 95–103.

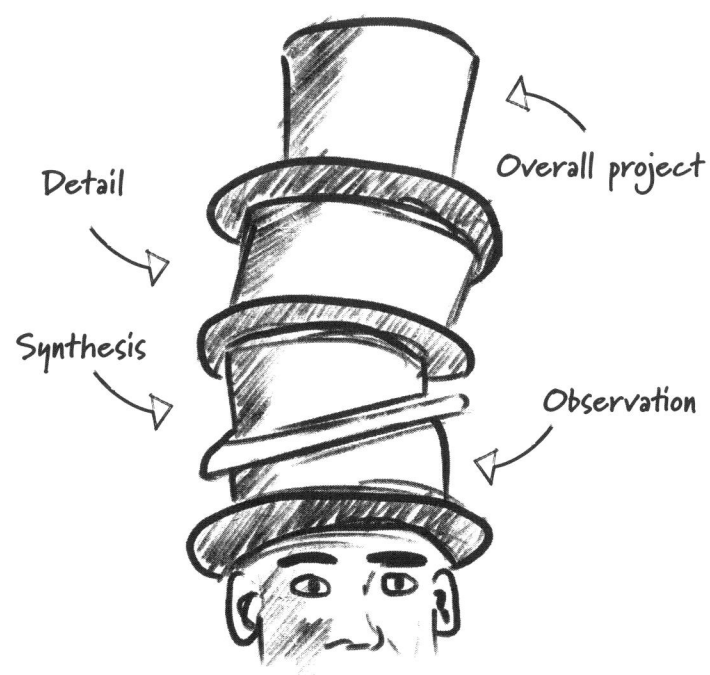

REFLECTION #2

TO MOVE BEYOND ASSUMPTIONS

Designers presented with the same design situation, in terms of assignment and information, in fact come up with the same conceptual design solution.[29]

- Find your boards, versions 1.0 to 2.0 (that contain your photos). Identify key insights. Back up your new findings with data (Quotes. Photos.)
- Find your first and second rounds of sketches. Identify key differences.

On the following pages, please make explicit the insights, surprises and anomalies you found, and back them up with data you have gathered during your research. For example, take a photo. Glue it in the book. Circle the details you notice, and write about them.
If you take a photo without processing it, you do not learn to 'see' properly. Marking and adding notes helps you interpret, see and place perspective on that photo. Reflect on how you do this and move beyond the immediate, the assumptions.

[29] Dorst, K., & Cross, N. (2001). Creativity in the design process: Co-evolution of problem–solution. Design Studies, 22(5), pp. 425–437.

REFLECTIONS:

Hmmmm...

LOOP I   IMMERSE • TO MOVE BEYOND ASSUMPTIONS

DAY 10
MILESTONE

- Partake in milestone.
- Capture feedback, and reflect on Milestone 1 in WS#11 Blind Spots.
- Note reflections/learning from the other presentation.

	IDEAS WORTH TRYING	REFLECTIONS / LEARNINGS
#1		
#2		
#3		

BLIND SPOTS

Write all the questions, comments and critiques you get in detail.

Work through them: Why are they asking this question? What does it concern? Is there something we did not think about? Is it a symptom of a larger problem or aspect we did not think about? What was received well or not so well? Which insights? Which solutions?

For example, the comment: 'I am not convinced a painter needs such a lamp.' Maybe your need is not specified enough? What does a painter need a lamp for? Maybe your problem is not a problem? Maybe the prioritisation of in your lamp does not solve a problem the painter currently has?
Figure out and really try to grasp what others see that you do not.

WRITE BLIND SPOTS HERE

-
-
-
-
-
-
-
-

Loop In

PROBE
USERS' REASONING

"The reflective practitioner allows himself to experience surprise, puzzlement or confusion in a situation which he finds uncertain or unique. He reflects on the phenomenon before him and on the prior understandings that have been implicit in his behaviour. He carries out an experiment which serves to generate both a new understanding of the phenomenon and a change in the situation'.

— Donald Schön

Notes

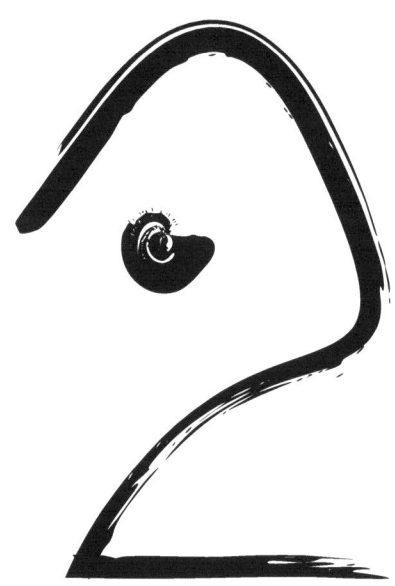

LOOP II **PROBE** USERS' REASONING

ROAD MAP

Road map 2*

Day 11 Mockups and style boards	Day 12 User probing	Day 13 User probing	Day 14 Storyboard + problem focus	Day 15 Experiments
Day 16 Experiments	Day 17 Prototypes	Day 18 Prototypes	Day 18 Storyboard, reflection and pitch prep	Day 20 Milestone II

*These are just suggestions. Remember to arrange or rearrange the day after what works and makes sense for your team.

WORKSHEETS
- WS#12 Prep + Plan
- WS#13 Mockup planning
- WS#14 Style board
- WS#15 User hooks and objections
- WS#16 Storyboard
- WS#17 Feasibility experiments
- WS#18 Usability experiments
- WS#19 Problem setting

REFLECTION
- R#3 Framing
- R#4 Co-development of problem and solution

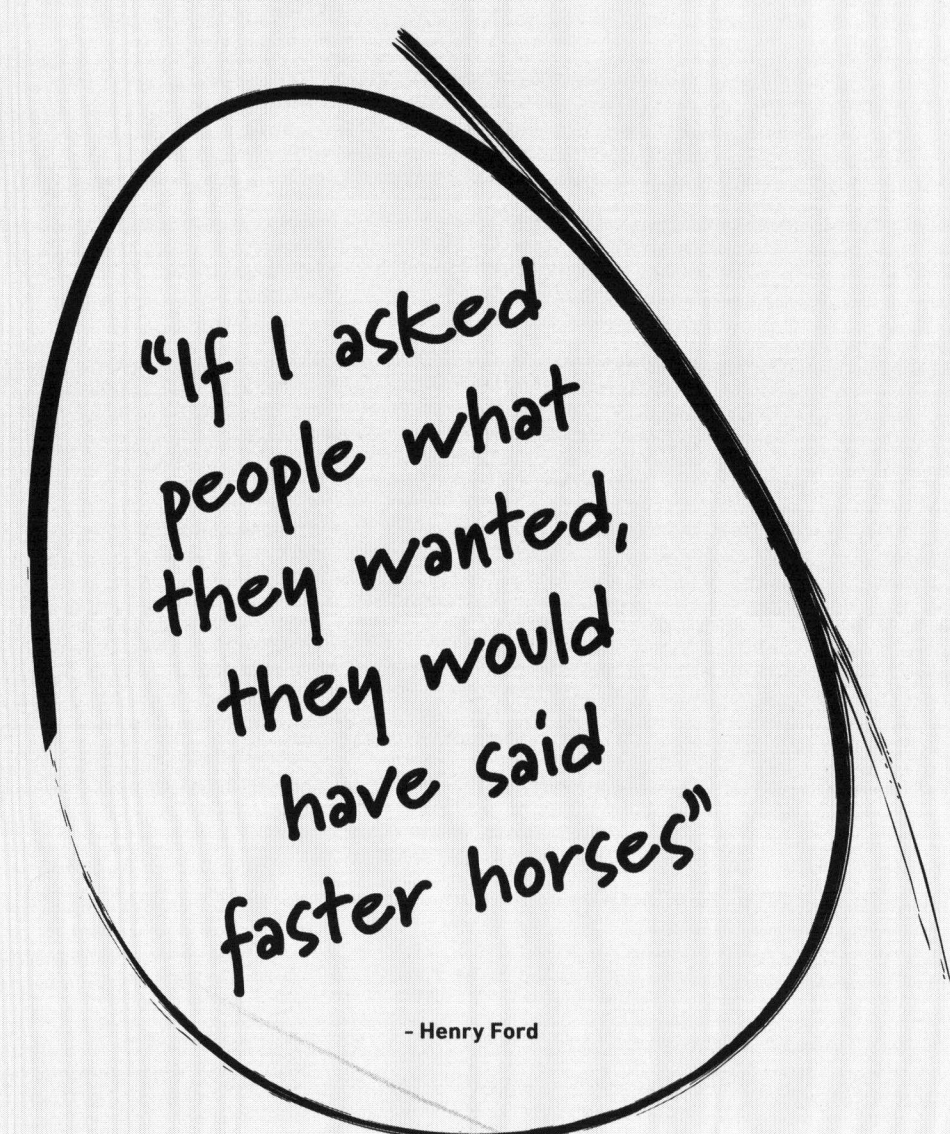

"If I asked people what they wanted, they would have said faster horses"

– Henry Ford

PROBE • USERS' REASONING

APPROACH: We know much about researching what is, but how do you research something that does not yet exist? A product that is to be? To research designs that do not yet exist, you need to move beyond the present situation and dive into user reasoning. You need to co-evolve the problem and solution to understand whether, how and in what way 'things' make sense.

HOOKS AND OBJECTIONS
In this work package, we provide a road map, worksheets and reflections that will help you understand users' reasoning. We mock up and play with users to examine hooks, objections and what we term polite indifference. Many books call it fail fast, to allow the fail to be made. We do not really care whether you fail, though we do care about understanding users' underlying rationale, their meaning making, and how they understand and make sense of the world.[30]
So, you may be able to design for their deepest aspirations, their latent needs and create value for their life. Design is in its essence not about you as a designer; we see us as the hands and minds of the people that help them create meaningful designs.

WHAT COULD BE
In Loop, I, we started with observations and interviews, but now, we quickly dig deeper into latent needs to understand what is meaningful to people (If you forgot, it may be useful to re-read the theory in brief on user research). Thus, we move from researching the present (as is) and move into poking the future, or what could be (to be). We look for missing links and outliers that we used to adjust our understanding of users' reasoning patterns. To design something users deeply desire, we need to examine their sense making. This helps us understand that how users make sense and design products that solve latent issues does not yet exist.

---

30 Krippendorff, K. (2005). The semantic turn: A new foundation for design. CRC Press.

THEORY IN BRIEF
We know much about how to observe, interview and understand users in their present (what has been or already is), but configuring research to get insights valuable for design is a completely different matter. In the second loop, the aim is to probe users' reasoning. We must understand the users' reasoning and design from that.

A cornerstone of design expertise is designers' ability to consider user sensemaking (i.e. how do they understand this product?). Some scholars, in fact, argue that the creation of meaning is the heart of designing. Krippendorf, in his book The Semantic Turn, argued: 'Humans do not see and act on the physical qualities of things, but on what they mean to them'.[31]

In our research of expert designers, we found the expert designers behind Lego Friends, the first successful girls' Lego product, who worked in quite an extraordinary manner on understanding users reasoning and creating new meaning from that.

In the past, LEGO had quite a number of girls' products. The products closest to the LEGO organisation's heart were rejected by the girls and vice versa; the products the girls loved were disregarded by LEGO as not 'real' LEGO products.

> 'This comes from the family ambition of being a toy company for both girls and boys, for all kids in the world, but it has been very much a company driven by, you know, doing toys for boys. We have had a lot of attempts for many years in the company, and we have not really cracked that.' (LEGO, manager)

The expert designers behind LEGO Friends spent years understanding what triggers girls. What do they hook on? What do they reject? What are their dreams and aspirations? What are their latent needs? Where and how do they thrive? But what surprised us the most was that they did the same with the LEGO organisation. What is LEGO? What do LEGO hook on? What do LEGO reject? What are the dreams and aspirations in LEGO? What are the latent needs in LEGO? Where and how do LEGO thrive? In the end, their brief became to make a truly LEGO and a truly girls' product:

---

31   Krippendorff, K. (2005). The semantic turn: A new foundation for design. CRC Press.

'We said it needs to be a 'truly LEGO experience' because, to me, it was one of the biggest issues before. All the girls' attempts we had at LEGO were not truly LEGO. Because we were doing bigger LEGO pieces, it was a different platform. It was not based on the existing LEGO brick platform. It was more complex and unique, and the process was more expensive. So, it is hard to have a sustainable platform for the future, for the many themes, many skills, many price points.' (LEGO, manager)

The secret to their success is how they dived into the reasoning of both the girls and the LEGO organisation. Instead of making a girls' LEGO product with a lot of special pieces, the LEGO organisation rejected it:

'So actually, 99% of the material, the bricks in the boxes, are the same bricks that we use in boys' products. It is more how the colours combine. So for, like, LEGO City, max, maybe there are three tones in there. They have the grey, they have the blue and the white, for instance if it is a police station. LEGO Friends, they are much more colourful. You have more colours going on: bright, detailed, rich in detail.

The main difference is the figures and animals, you know, the figures, they have to be detailed, more realistic. That is the reason we did a new figure platform, but the animals. There is a reason we also have to develop a new element for animals for girls. It is the importance of the facial expression of them, they have to be, you know, super, super cute and with details on their faces.' (LEGO, manager)

It is about making a perfect match between LEGO and the girls, a truly LEGO product and a truly girls' product, a girls' product that tapped into LEGO's DNA

DAY 11

MOCKUPS AND STYLEBOARDS

INSTRUCTION
- Video C: Probe to understand sense making
- Video 4: Mockups
- Video 5: Style boards of aspirational products

TEAMWORK

Aim
Familiarise yourself with your team, the task and the Loop II material.

Process
Read Loop II (including the intro, theory, road map II, boards and the reflection.)
- [ ] While reading, note what needs to be arranged and practicalities (e.g. contact users and plan beforehand, remember a long day, bring a camera etc.). Individually note questions and problems you have during this loop. WS#13

Share insights from reading Loop II.
- [ ] Write a collective mind map of arrangements, practicalities, questions and problems in Loop II.
- [ ] Distribute the tasks on the list between you. Individuals volunteer to take todo tasks and help each other find solutions to challenges. Brainstorm, write on sticky notes, and agree on a preliminary answer/solution that will help you move forward.

TEAMWORK

Aim
Attempt to fully understand the solution space with a minimum of eight mockups.

Process:
Based on the prior work and feedback plan, develop eight mockups. WS#14. Remember to make them as diverse as possible to increase learning. We are looking for insights into where the nerves of the design might be. Thus, we are probing for hooks and objections, love and rejection. The only thing we do not want is polite indifference, which will push your design off on a completely boring track.

INDIVIDUAL WORK

Each person creates a style board with a style direction. WS#15. Look at aspirational products that you from the user test find the users aspire to (not in your product category, but in across product categories). What are your users' aspirational products? Try to understand the essence of these. Consider eight aesthetic directions. Make the board with loose photos users may pick during the user probe.

PRACTICE-IN-BRIEF

Please listen to the B&O case podcast.
https://www.amcopenhagen.com/designkan/design-kan-drive-strategier-bo/

WORKSHEET

WS#12 PREP AND PLAN

Start here by noting tasks, aspects and considerations that come to mind while going through the road map, worksheets and reflection on Loop 1.

Designed by: _____ Date: _____ Iteration #: _____

User research arrangement:
Who, how, where, what?

Linda Nhu Laursen and Louise Møller Haase (2022) Designerly Loops.

Ideas/opportunities:
Note anything that comes to your mind your contacts/resources/etc.

Materials list:
What do we need each day.

Challenges/obstacles:
Note anything that comes to your mind.

Other:
Issues to remember or you came to think of.

WORKSHEET

WS#13 MOCKUP PLANNING

Stretch the solution space, think about different sizes, functions, ergonomics, features – and ensure you have a mockup at each end of the spectrum for each parameter, for example mockups in different sizes, with different interaction forms, with different functions and different placements. Think about different media and what to use them for, for example mockups in paper (for rapid testing of print, patterns, interactions, colours), mockups in foam (for testing ergonomics, soft and round shapes and curves, it takes some time) and mockups in cardboard (for testing size, dimensions, moveable parts) etc.

Designed by: _____ Date: _____ Iteration #: _____

Write three aspects of testing (e.g. a round button, a huge long light and a carry strap).	Draw the plan for the mockup in this tile. Here, you specify the media.

Linda Nhu Laursen and Louise Møller Haase (2022) Designerly Loops.

Write three aspects of testing (e.g. a round button, a huge long light and a carry strap)

Draw the plan for the mockup in this tile. Here, you specify the media

WORKSHEET

WS#14 STYLEBOARD

Consider the aspirations of the user – what do they aspire to?

For example, being perceived as a highly educated expert (e.g. dentist tool expression), being perceived as a formidable worker (e.g. power tools) or being perceived as an artist (e.g. artisanship utensils, such as the paintbrush).

Designed by: _____   Date: _____   Iteration #: _____

Aspiration:

Place style 'a' here. _____

Linda Nhu Laursen and Louise Møller Haase (2022) Designerly Loops.

Aspiration:

Place style 'b' here.

Aspiration:

Place style 'c' here.

DAY 12+13
USER PROBING

TEAMWORK

Aim: Identify what concept directions the users find most important/relevant and irrelevant/meaningless. Test them on diverse users.

Process:
- [ ] Show the users the style board, and let them reflect on it. Ask them to pick a photo they like the most, and ask them to imagine the mockup is made in this style/material.
- [ ] Present each of the mockups for users, one at a time. Be active listeners; be curious and question to understand their perspective. The aim is not to get the user to choose the best prototype. Instead, the aim is to learn what is interesting, great, exciting, despicable, irrelevant or meaningless in every prototype. In other words, we are looking for what they hook onto or object to. We are looking for the nerve in design.
- [ ] Collect all the insights from the user test. Make a hook and rejections worksheet (WS#16) for each user.

WORKSHEET

WS#15 USER HOOKS AND OBJECTIONS

THE AIM IS TO HIT: THE NERVE IN DESIGN

USER NAME: _____

HOOKS
When users really hook on a product, it is typically because it has some novelty in the way it solves an unexpressed need. Then your job is just to figure out what was actually the hook and make it sharper, more apparent. Make different versions and interpretations of it. You'll likely learn that your first interpretation was faulty. Hooks capture what makes a product meaningful in the eyes of that user.

OBJECTIONS
When we look for objections, we find not only what on the surface does not work or is unattractive. Objections typically emerge when framing proposals go against the opinions of the users. Objections are the flip side of hooks and they are just as valuable to discover. You should use these as fuel to flip your concept around.

INDIFFERENCE
If users are polite, indifferent, not wanting to buy or criticise your mockups, you have been too safe. You stayed within the present. Put your mockups on the shelf, and go further!

Linda Nhu Laursen and Louise Møller Haase (2022) Designerly Loops.

THE AIM IS TO HIT: THE NERVE IN DESIGN

USER NAME: _____

HOOKS

OBJECTIONS

INDIFFERENCE

THE AIM IS TO HIT: THE NERVE IN DESIGN

USER NAME: _____

HOOKS

OBJECTIONS

INDIFFERENCE

Linda Nhu Laursen and Louise Møller Haase (2022) Designerly Loops.

THE AIM IS TO HIT: THE NERVE IN DESIGN
USER NAME: _____

HOOKS

OBJECTIONS

INDIFFERENCE

STORYTELLING TIME

DAY 14
STORYBOARD + PROBLEM FOCUS

INDIVIDUAL WORK

Aim
Every team member redevelops a storyboard, based on user insight.

Process
- [ ] The individual development of a storyboard (WS#17). Really zoom in on a particular aspect, problem, situation or circumstance. We do not want a general one, but rather, one that reveals a hidden story that you did not notice before your user research.

TEAMWORK

Aim
Build a joint storyboard

Process
- [ ] Share your individual storyboards. Discuss variances. Why are they different? How can we agree on what to focus on? Develop an integrated storyboard.

TEAMWORK

Aim
To define a central problem by reviewing and reflecting on hooks, objections and indifference from the user probe.

Process
- [ ] Review the worksheets of hooks and objections for each concept. Try to make sense of what to do. Try to combine concepts, work with particular concepts etc.
  Note and reflect on which solutions are not worth progressing and why.
- [ ] Based on the storyboard and the user insights, now decide in which direction to move. In some cases, you might find a particularly strong concept where partial solution principles are added from another concept. Write them down. In other cases, you need to come up with/combine more concepts. Base these on your user tests. What did the users find most important, relevant, and exciting versus irrelevant and unimportant?

WS#16 STORYBOARD

Think about where to zoom in on the story. Where do we place our attention? What is the hidden story we have not seen before? How do we frame this? Use the storyboard to focus on and dive into a very important hidden layer.
In this loop, storyboards are used for trying out concepts and ideas, that is, getting an idea of how the concept may unfold over time. How does the solution fit the situation? The problem? It is a synthesis tool to co-evolve the criteria and provisional design.[32]

Designed by: _____   Date: _____   Iteration #: _____

Focus on drawing out key problems

1	2
3	4

---

[32] Roozenburg, N. F., & Eekels, J. (1995). Product design: Fundamentals and methods.

5 _____	6 _____
7 _____	8 _____
9 _____	10 _____

DAY 15 + 16

EXPERIMENTS

INSTRUCTION
- Video 6: Light studies for feasibility (5 min., ML, MH, LL)
- Video 7: Bodystorming for usability (5 min., ML, MH, LL)

TEAMWORK

Aim
To settle the design usability and feasibility arena through important considerations.

Process

☐ Perform usability studies. Conduct three bodystorming sessions where you take a product-to-be (prototype) and try/play with scenarios. Select key scenarios and critical points, and try out a conceptual prototype of all of these. (WS#18) For example, how would you set it up? How would you use it? Take photos of it, and get a feel of the dimensions, priorities, focus – what is desirable for the user?
Compare the bodystorming to the storyboard. Look at it as an 'as is' and a 'to be/ could be' to understand the value you may create.

☐ Do three feasibility studies. (WS#19) For example, if you are designing a lamp, do a light study of light sources to see if they work, technically speaking. Do the light sources fill the requirements?

SKETCH:

WORKSHEET

WS#17 FEASIBILITY EXPERIMENTS

What feasibility aspects are important for your product? Light, battery life, waterproofing? Plan which experiments to do (remember to take photos), and then capture what you have learned.

Designed by: _____ Date: _____ Iteration #: _____

EXPERIMENT ON:

EXPERIMENT ON:

EXPERIMENT ON:

Linda Nhu Laursen and Louise Møller Haase (2022) Designerly Loops.

EXPERIMENT ON:

_____
_____

EXPERIMENT ON:

_____
_____

EXPERIMENT ON:

_____
_____

EXPERIMENT ON:

_____
_____

WS#18 USABILITY EXPERIMENTS

What usability aspects are important for your product? Size, weight, grabbing mechanism? Plan which experiments to do (remember to take photos), and then capture your lessons.

Designed by: _____ Date: _____ Iteration #: _____

EXPERIMENT ON:

EXPERIMENT ON:

EXPERIMENT ON:

Linda Nhu Laursen and Louise Møller Haase (2022) Designerly Loops.

EXPERIMENT ON:

_____

_____

EXPERIMENT ON:

_____

_____

EXPERIMENT ON:

_____

_____

EXPERIMENT ON:

_____

_____

SKETCH:

… IMMERSE • TO MOVE BEYOND ASSUMPTIONS

DAY 17+18+19
PROTOTYPING

INSTRUCTION Video 8: Prototyping Manner and Means

TEAMWORK

Aim
Bring the concept together (physical and virtual)

Process
☐ Make prototypes in the manner that fits the means, for example physical for size, 3D for looks, other products for mechanical principles.

TEAMWORK

Aim
Problem setting. Review your work so far. Research, insights, problems, solutions. Make the reflections. Gather the relevant and important pieces of your work to date, and weave them into a storyline for a presentation of the design pitch.

Process
☐ Make a problem setting (WS#20) where you collect all the revelations in your process and your deeper understanding of the users, context, product/market, products in time (storyboard) and evolution of the concept sketch-to-mockup-to-prototypes.
☐ Reflect on your practice and your understanding of how you framed the user's reasoning.
☐ Reflect on your practice and the co-development of a problem and solution.

WORKSHEET

WS#19 PROBLEM SETTING

Collect and review all the insights and 'aha' moments you collected during the process, one perspective at a time. In the third column, draw/note problems and insights.

Designed by: _____   Date: _____   Iteration #: _____

	1.0 (assumptions)	2.0 (insights)	Problem or idea element
User (Personas boards)			
Context			
Product before your user research– market			
In time (Story- boards)			
Body storming			
Light experiments			

Linda Nhu Laursen and Louise Møller Haase (2022) Designerly Loops.

	1.0 (assumptions)	2.0 (insights)	Problem or idea element
User (Personas boards)			
Context			
Product before your user research–market			
In time (Storyboards)			
Body storming			
Light experiments			

REFLECTION #3
FRAMING[33]

Framing is a key methodological approach within design. During the design process, which is a reflective practice, the designer frames or reframes the design situation.[34] Framing serves as a hypothesis or as a direction for the design project, which is then explored. Buchanan described framing as a source of new ideas and opportunities.[35] Framing helps to rephrase a problem or a situation, which is thereby extended beyond the obvious to determine whether the problem is an actual symptom of another problem and, eventually, to identify the core of both the problem and the solution.[36]

Please write how you have framed your problem in different ways during the project. Write down your problems.

How has your understanding of the problem changed during the project? ('What did the user say vs. what the user actually needs?' 'Why didn't concept X work, and what key takeaways are to be transferred to the next concept?')

---

[33] Laursen & Haase (2019). The shortcomings of design thinking when compared to designerly thinking, The Design Journal.
[34] Schön, D. A. (1987). Educating the reflective practitioner.
[35] Buchanan, R. (1992). Wicked problems in design thinking. Design Issues, 8(2), 5–21.
[36] Dorst, K. (2011). The core of 'design thinking' and its application. Design Studies, 32(6), 521–532.

REFLECTIONS:

REFLECTION #4
CO-DEVELOPMENT OF THE PROBLEM AND SOLUTION[37]

The co-development of a problem and solution is another core methodological approach in design[38]. It is the standard process involved in most problem solving, as designers engage in an iterative process of suggesting and evaluating proposals, wherein a greater understanding of both the problem and the solution emerges.[39]

---

[37] Laursen & Haase (2019). The shortcomings of design thinking when compared to designerly thinking, The Design Journal.
[38] Cross, N. (2006). Design as a discipline. Designerly Ways of Knowing, pp. 95–103.
[39] Dorst, K., & Cross, N. (2001). Creativity in the design process: Co-evolution of problem–solution. Design Studies, 22(5), pp. 433.

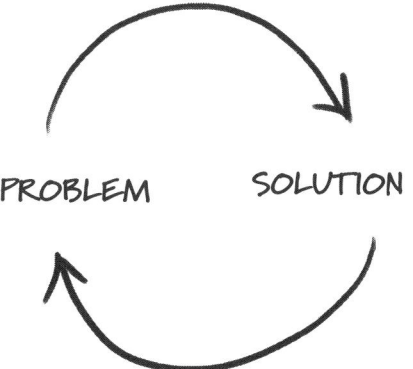

DAY 20
MILESTONE

- Partake in milestone
- Capture feedback, and reflect on Milestone 2 in WS#19 Blind Spots.
- Note reflections and lessons from the other presentation.

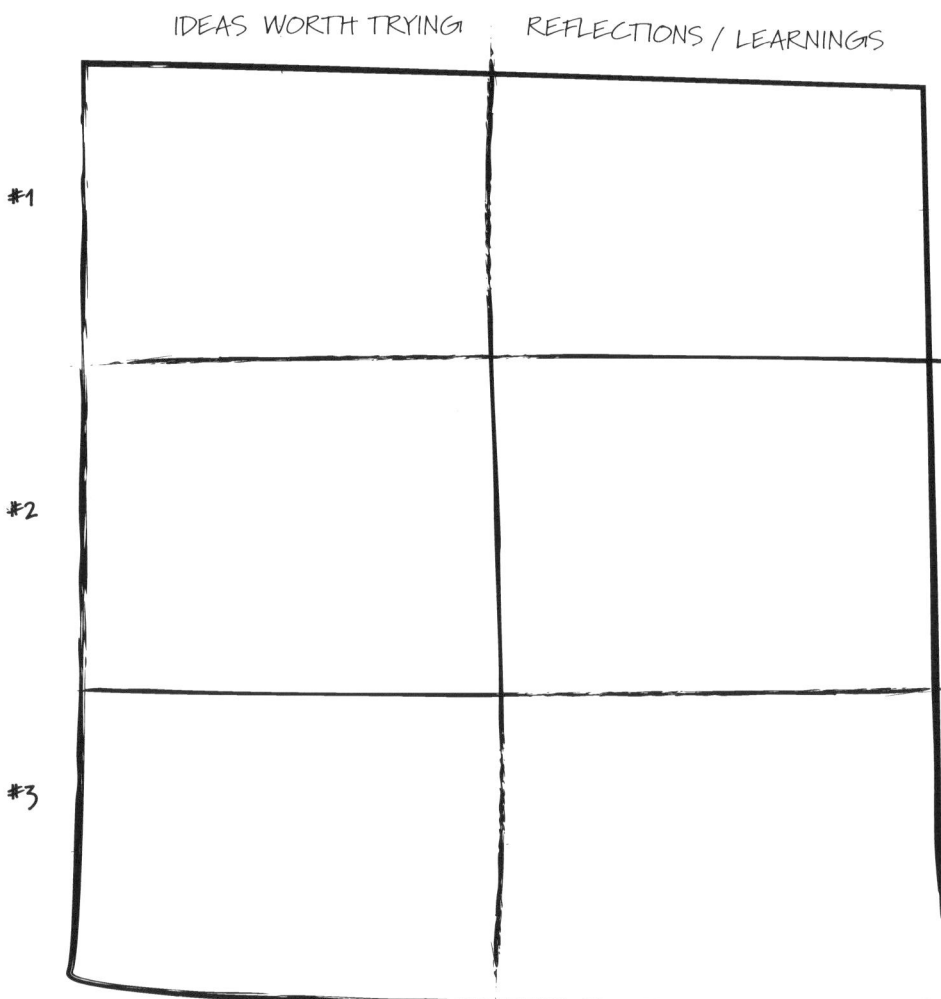

BLIND SPOTS

Write down all the questions, comments and critiques you get in detail. Work through them: Why are they asking this question? What does it concern? Is there something we did not think about? Is it a symptom of a larger problem/aspect we did not think about? Which of the insights? Which of the solutions were recived well/not so well?

WRITE BLIND SPOTS HERE

-
-
-
-
-
-
-
-

PERSIST
UNTIL ALL THE DOTS ARE CONNECTED

Loop III

"The designer may take account of unintended changes he has made in the situation by forming new appreciations and understandings and by making new moves. He shapes the situation under his initial appreciation of it, the situation "talks back", and he responds to the situation's back talk'

— **Donald Schön**

Notes

LOOP III   **PERSIST** UNTIL ALL THE DOTS ARE CONNECTED

ROAD MAP

*Road map 3**

Day 21 Demands and wishesz	Day 22 Deconstruct to understand elements and structures	Day 23 Deconstruct to define elements and structures	Day 24 Prototype parts, 1.0, 2.0...	Day 25 Prototype parts, 1.0, 2.0...
Day 26 Prototype parts, 1.0, 2.0...	Day 27 Prototype parts, 1.0, 2.0...	Day 28 Prototype parts, 1.0, 2.0...	Day 29 Prototype parts, 1.0, 2.0...	Day 30 Prototype parts, 1.0, 2.0...

*These are just suggestions. Remember to arrange or rearrange the day after what works and makes sense for your team.

WORKSHEETS
- ☐ WS#22 Prep and Plan
- ☐ WS#23 Demands and Wishes
- ☐ WS#24 Product Disassembly Analysis
- ☐ WS#25 Prototypes

REFLECTION
- ☐ Reflection #5 Solution-led goal analysis
- ☐ Reflection #6 Persist

LOOP III

PERSIST • UNTIL ALL THE DOTS ARE CONNECTED

APPROACH: To bridge the void between ideas, a concept sketch and a real product you can touch and use. You need to keep on driving the design process. You need to move from details to structures, from elements to the whole. You need to find all missing links and persist until all the elements are tied together, until all the dots are connected. Then reality will speak for itself.

CONCEPTUALISING MEANS CONNECTING
When you have a clear concept in your head, there is still some way to go to make it real. Lots of elements and contradicting aspects need to fit together. We believe there is much more to this than making it physical; it is where every curve, material and function that each solves different needs come together as a whole. You need to tie aspects together, give them matter, give them means. Understand how they may be constructed and what material they may be made of. Figure out what the demands are. Do you need to put it under water, or do you often drop the product? How much space does the stuff inside actually take up? What is the price? How does it fit in user homes?

Interaction

Expression

THE CHALLENGES IN MAKING THINGS REAL
When you find a solution that solves one problem, it often creates a new one. For example, when you construct a tall structure, that stands very stably, it may be difficult to move and fold together. So many important aspects, details and perspectives need to be considered. To create a great design, we need to understand the challenges in making it real. Gravity. Price. Material. Construction. Interaction. You name it. You, as designers, need the entire practical palette here, while you keep prioritising from needs, hopes, aspirations. It is about detailing elements, taking different perspectives, understanding important aspects and difficult tensions, and tying them together in a coherent whole, where every little piece fits. And more importantly, you need to do it repeatedly until the design is real and the intent and every detail fit together. Not until you have improved the design numerous times will it be worthy. When concepts face reality, we have to persist until all the dots are connected.

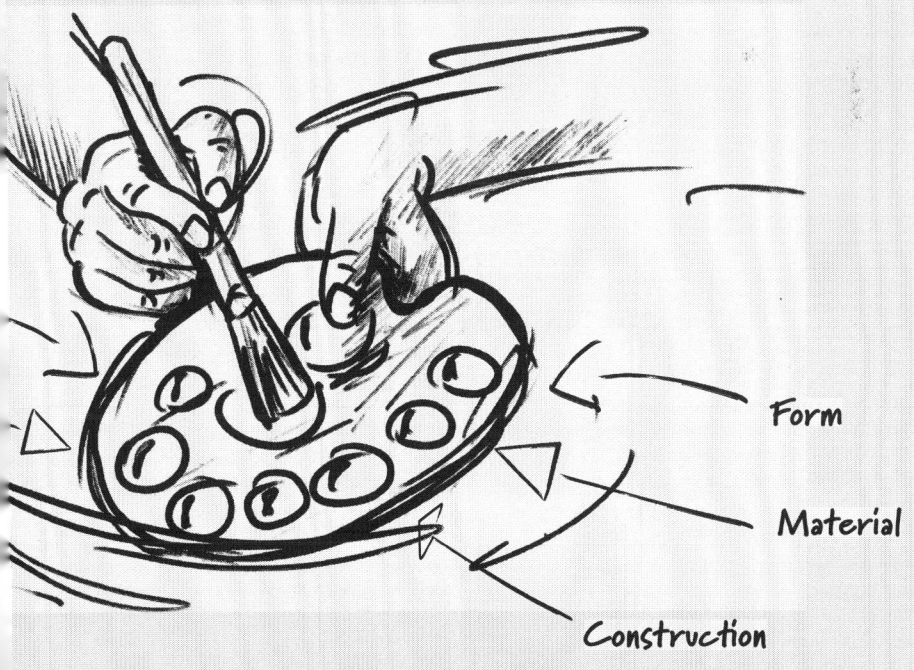

THEORY IN BRIEF

At its essence, design is a wicked problem, that is a problem that is the opposite of tame. It has no right or wrong, like maths where 2+2 = 4. In design, we have only solutions that are better or worse. There is no limit or definitive conditions; numerous solutions are possible.[40] Therefore, there are no right or logical ways to cope with such problems. You need to abduct your way out of it.[41]

Abduction is basically 'proposal making', making a probable conclusion from what you presently know. But that does not mean designers believe their first proposal works or is the right proposal. They use their proposal to learn from it; to figure out what was wrong. When design experts deduct, they engage in a *dialogue with the situation.* The creation of models, sketches and prototypes is a key approach for designers to capture their tacit knowledge and interpretation of the design situation and transform it into testable proposals.[42]
Thus, the creation of physical artefacts, such as sketches, models and prototypes, is central to utilising 'intuitive knowing in the midst of action'.[43] It allows designers to utilise their tacit knowledge through engaging in a dialogue with the matter, a 'conversation' with the situation, where they reflect while doing as well as on decisions about the next step—reflection in and on action.[44]

---

40 Rittel, H. W., & Webber, M. M. (1973). Dilemmas in a general theory of planning. Policy Sciences, 4(2), pp. 155-169.
41 Buchanan, R. (1992). Wicked problems in design thinking. Design Issues, 8(2), pp. 5-21.
42 Cross, N. (1982). Designerly ways of knowing. Design Studies, 3(4), pp. 221-227.
43 Schön, D. (1938). The reflective practitioner. New York, 1083.
44 Schön, D. (1938). The reflective practitioner. New York, 1083.

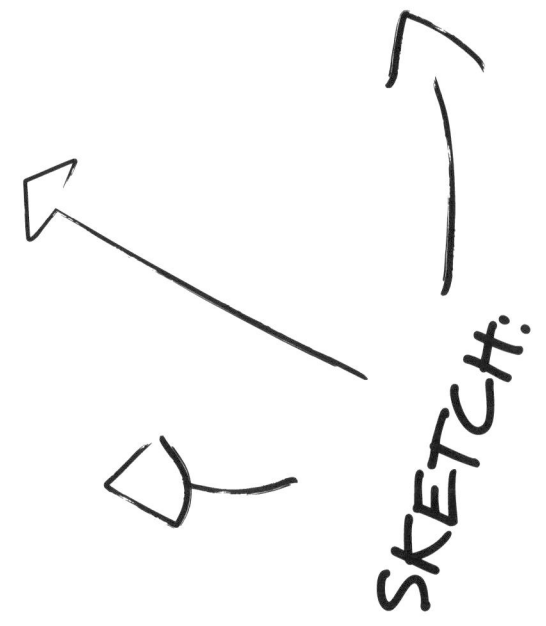

DAY 21
DEMANDS AND WISHES

ON YOUR TEAM

Aim
Familiarise yourself with Work Package III.

Process
- [ ] Read Road Map III.
- [ ] Note what needs to be arranged and practicalities (e.g. prototyping and what to plan beforehand, remember to bring materials, etc.; WS#22)
- [ ] Note opportunities and challenges during this work package.
- [ ] Please also review personal aspirations, ambitions, investments, efforts and practicalities.

INSTRUCTIONS

Video d: Persists until all the dots are connected
Video 9: Demands and Wishes

TEAMWORK

Aim
Identify demands and wishe

Process
- [ ] Go over all the boards. Off the top of your head, brainstorm and write any initial requirements and needs that come to your mind on top of them, such as the need to be 'easy to carry'.
- [ ] Do a first translation of demands and wishes (WS#23). For example, with 'easy to carry', what do we mean by being easy to carry? We mean one man should be able to carry it with one hand. Then look at each of the needs, demands and wishes and specify them further. That means xx kg and a max xx size, and sets demands for a way to carry it.
- [ ] Do a preliminary demand specification.

WORKSHEET

WS#20 PREP AND PLAN

Start here by noting tasks, aspects and considerations that come to your mind while going through the road map, worksheets and reflection of Loop 1.

Designed by: _____ Date: _____ Iteration #: _____

User research arrangement:
Whom, How, Where, What?

Linda Nhu Laursen and Louise Møller Haase (2022) Designerly Loops.

Ideas/opportunities:
Note anything that comes to your mind your contacts/resources/etc

Materials list:
What do we need each day.

Challenges/obstacles:
Note anything that comes to your mind

Other:
Issues to remember or you came to think of

WS#21 DEMANDS AND WISHES

Brainstorm and specify your demand and wish in a tree such as this.

Designed by: _____ Date: _____ Iteration #: _____

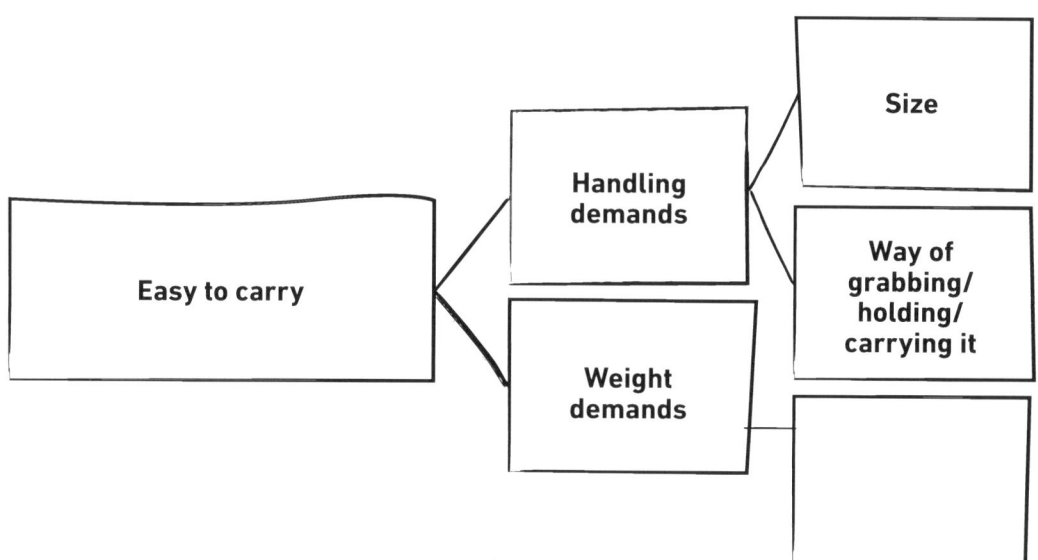

Linda Nhu Laursen and Louise Møller Haase (2022) Designerly Loops.

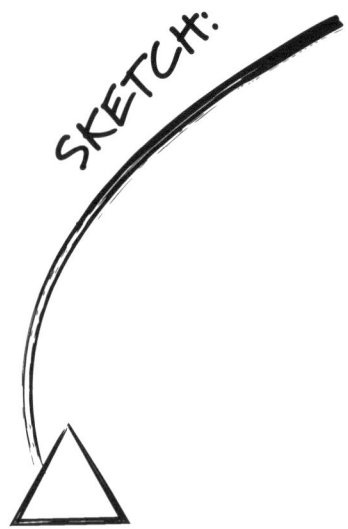

DAY 22+23
DECONSTRUCT TO UNDERSTAND ELEMENTS AND STRUCTURES

INSTRUCTIONS | Video 10: Deconstruct a product to understand their integration

TEAMWORK

Aim
Learn how elements integrate feasibility, desirability and usability.

Process
- [ ] Disassemble products to dive into their construction, elements, material and connection. (WS#24)
- [ ] Draw an expanded view, or glue the elements up in an expanded view.
- [ ] Note the elements, their size, shape and material, and try to understand the purpose of each element. Learn from it and why it is designed as it is. Understand the limitations and solution principles of the type of products you are designing.

TEAMWORK

Aim
Draw components to understand construction + materials.
Chooseelements, construction principles and materials.

Process
- [ ] Each person develops a proposal for a construction principle, where the placement of each element is considered (also black boxes). Model work is encouraged.
- [ ] Discussion of the different principles and the final concept.

WORKSHEET

WS#22 PRODUCT DISSASSEMBLY ANALYSIS

Note the elements' size, shape and material, and try to understand the purpose of each element. Learn from it and why it is designed as it is. Understand the limitations and solution principles of the type of products you are designing. Identify elements, components' sizes, construction principles, material demands etc.

Designed by: _____ Date: _____ Iteration #: _____

Linda Nhu Laursen and Louise Møller Haase (2022) Designerly Loops.

SKETCH:

LOOP III   IMMERSE • TO MOVE BEYOND ASSUMPTIONS

DAY 24-30
PROTOTYPE PARTS 1.0, 2.0...

INSTRUCTIONS | Video 11: Prototyping Parts 1.0, 2.0

TEAMWORK

Aim
Increase the maturation of the design. Develop and integrate its construction, usability and desirability.

Process
- [ ] Individually work on sketches and proposals for different aspects: first, materials; second, construction; third, interaction; and fourth, expression. Consider diverse elements, connections between them, and the like. Take 20 minutes to individually research and sketch a proposal of each aspect. Take one theme at a time. Pick themes relevant to your product.
- [ ] Pick and share the best principal proposals. Plan and prototype them. (WS#25)
- [ ] Start making prototypes of critical parts of the products, such as the mechanical part, the interaction, the base, and the folding mechanism.
- [ ] Then, make more advanced prototypes of the entire product. (WS#25) Consider the construction principle, the usability, the materials, the stability, the expression etc. Move from the details to the architecture, connection and assembly.
- [ ] Remember to evaluate the pros and cons of the prototype. The purpose is to learn from mistakes and refine your design.
- [ ] Think about which material is relevant or makes the most sense to prototype (Virtual and Physical 2D, 3D). Some of you may 3D print the interior technology you may visualise on the computer.
- [ ] You might also buy a product and use its parts, learn about the material, function, size and structure of the different parts. You are not making a calculated or production mature design; instead, the aim is to show probable realisation. If an Ikea product for 30 kr can hold this piece, take this heat and have this strength, we argue it may also work in our product.

WORKSHEET

WS#23 PROTOTYPE

Designed by: _____   Date: _____   Iteration #: _____

Focus:
What do you want to understand?
Which part/aspect of the product are you prototyping?

Fidelity:
What do your prototype need to do?

Materials list:
What do you need to build it?

Prototype sketch:
Draw the prototype here

Learnings:
Write here what you know and what you don't know.

Place photo here

REFLECTION #5

SOLUTION-LED GOAL ANALYSIS[45]

Designs do not spend much time qualifying the goal. Instead, the focus is on identifying the right solution[46] and ensuring that the identified solution is meaningful to both the users and the context.[47] This approach involves searching for a deeper understanding of users' aspirations, values and priorities. It is about identifying a path towards the most desirable future.[48] It also means that the goal may be subject to changes along the way.

On the following pages, please reflect on the solutions you proposed and the learnings they provided. First, draw a timeline, and then as mini thumbnails, note key solutions. Then, with a coloured pen, write down the insights that came from proposals and how they changed the direction for the proposals along the way.

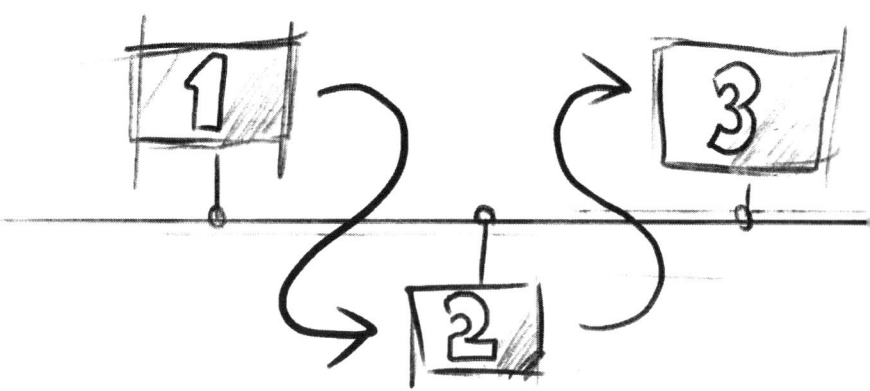

---

45 Laursen & Haase (2019). The shortcomings of design thinking when compared to designerly thinking, The Design Journal.
46 Cross, N. (2006). Design as a discipline, Designerly Ways of Knowing, pp. 95–103.
47 Krippendorff, K. (2006). The semantic turn: A new foundation for design. CRC Press.
48 Dorst, K. (2011). The core of 'design thinking' and its application. Design Studies, 32(6), 521–532.

REFLECTIONS:

REFLECTION #6

PERSIST

The hard thing about persisting is persisting. It may at times feel like you are going around in circles. Other times, it may feel like you have to start over, and you might be frustrated because, if you just had seen the writing on the wall from the beginning, you would have avoided so much excessive work. Or when everything is aligned, you find one missing link that ruins your clear pattern. (However, if your process has been polished and linear, you have not searched hard enough for missing links. They are probably still there. Go look for them before they come chasing you.)

On this page, please list your setbacks in bullet form, based on the previous timeline. When you felt lost. Hit a wall. Where your direction or concept seemed to fall on its face. All your blind spots and the things you overlooked.
Now, we know you do not want to do this at this point, but now, write down the five weakest points in your current solution. Question yourself: Why do they still exist?

REFLECTIONS:

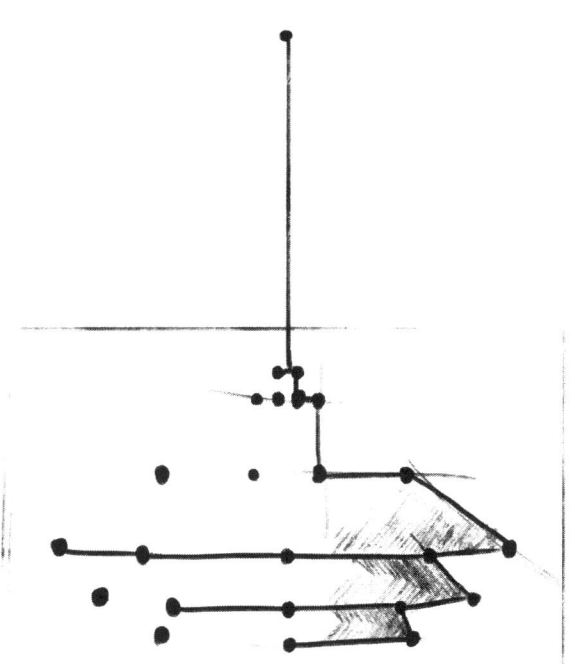

Loop IV

REFLECT
TO STORYTELL THE POSITION

'Professionals have been disturbed to find that they cannot account for processes they have come to see as central to professional competence. It is difficult for them to imagine how to describe and teach what might be meant by making sense of uncertainty, performing artistically, setting problems, and choosing among competing professional paradigms, when these processes seem mysterious in the light of the prevailing model of professional knowledge. We are bound to an epistemology of practice which leaves us at a loss to explain, or even to describe, the competences to which we now give overriding importance'.

— Donald Schön

Sketch

LOOP III   **REFLECT** TO STORYTELL A POSITION

ROAD MAP

Road map 4

Day 31 Reflect on the storyline and position	Day 32 Reflect on the storyline and position	Day 33 Last round of reflection, storytelling and prototyping	Day 34 Last round of reflection, storytelling and prototyping	Day 35 Last round of reflection, storytelling and prototyping
Day 36 Last round of reflection, storytelling and prototyping	Day 37 Last round of reflection, storytelling and prototyping	Day 38 Last round of reflection, storytelling and prototyping	Day 39 Last round of reflection, storytelling and prototyping	Day 40 Delivery

REFLECTION
- ☐ R#7 Modal Shift
- ☐ R#8 Framing
- ☐ R#9 Co-development of the problem and solution
- ☐ R#10 Dialogue with the situation
- ☐ R#11 Solution-led goal analysis
- ☐ R#12 Reflective practice

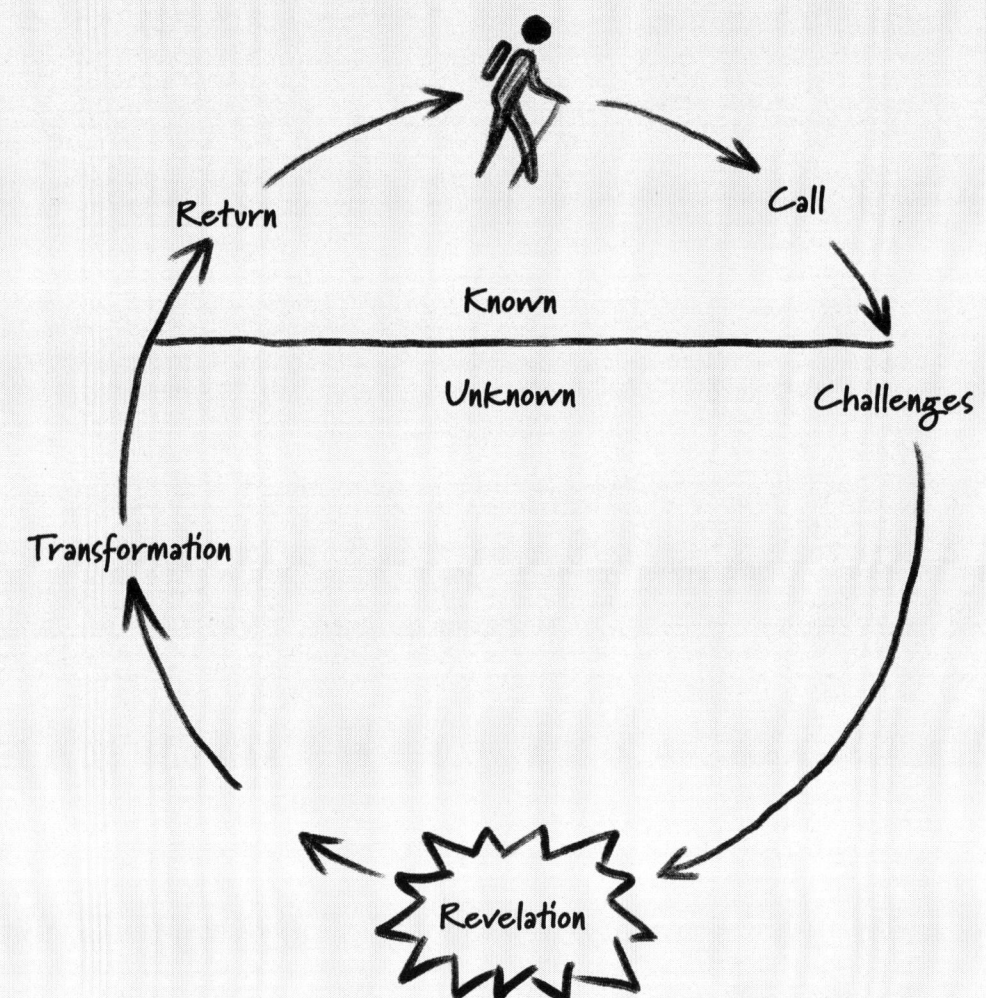

REFLECT TO STORYTELL A POSITION

When you have a design, a concept, there is still some way to go to make it impactful; you need to crystallise it and explain its significance. This fourth loop aims at reflection to help build your argumentation of the product (and process): moving from abstract to concrete, from details to structure, from decisions to priorities. Tie it together in a meaningful manner. We reflect and use storytelling to tie fragments and elements together into a meaningful explanation of a product's raison d'être, or reason for being. In this loop, we work with the design's position in the world. Is it important? Is it impactful? Does it make a difference in this world, to someone? Or is it yet another product that we do not need?

THE MOTIVATION BEHIND THE DESIGN
Thus, the fourth loop is in design, as conceptual as the first three; it is not just about communication. It is about framing and reflection. In this loop, we create a compelling positioning, an argumentation for the product. In this loop, we work with the worth and value of our design. Why is the design significant? What is its intent and meaning? What motivates the design? Through storytelling, we tie the problem to the solution. Details and decisions are placed into a meaningful structure. These loops answer whether we made a worthy design.

YOU MAY EXPERIENCE IT AS CHAOTIC, BUT TELL IT CLEARLY
Moreover, this loop is about reflection on your previous actions. Throughout the loops, you have reflected on actions, missing links and surprises. In this loop, we want you to look backwards again. This will help you crystallise your design vision as well as provide you with learning that will help you move up the skills acquisition ladder to progress your designerly expertise. As the Danish philosopher Kierkegaard famously said, 'Life can only be understood backwards, but it must be lived forward'. The approach of this book is inspired by the many design experts we studied who are mostly due to think and think to do. The doing and reflection of design is central for them; it is a means to progress the design and move up an experience level.

In this loop, we tie the beginning to the end.

DAYS 31-32
REFLECT ON THE STORYLINE AND POSITION.2.0...

INSTRUCTIONS
- Video e: Storytell to create positioning.
- Video 12: Prototype for integration.

Process
Read Loop IV (includes reading the intro, theory, road map IV and the reflection). While reading, note what needs to be arranged and practicalities. Note questions you have for this loop.

TEAMWORK

Aim
Reflect on your process in creating the storyline.

Process
- [ ] Go through the process loop by loop.
- [ ] Divide into smaller groups of two or three people.
- [ ] First, collect all research and documentation (photos, interviews etc.) and all the design development documentation from all the loops, irst loops I, II, III and then IV. Lay it out on the floor with the actions in chronological order.
- [ ] Write down insights (that is, the observations you used to progress your design). Now, write down each design action and what you learned from it. Write surprises, revelations and aha moments, as well as setbacks and challenges down on paper.
- [ ] Take a photo of it – this is the sketch structure for the content of each loop, the basic storyline.

TEAM DISCUSSION

Aim
Reflect on your storyline to create a position.

Process

- [ ] In smaller groups, find themes/topics that are characteristic and imperative to each design loop. Try to identify the one overarching/key theme for your design and the typically 1–2 issues from each loop that support it. These are typically not apparent from the beginning, but you identify them along the way.

    For example, in a conventional chick flick, the primary theme would be the search for true love. Underneath that, you find several issues (e.g. the ability to put yourself out there on the dating market, at dinners and at dances), enhancing one's appearance (clothes, manners, habits), getting rid of a bad social climate (the bad friend) etc.

- [ ] Now, in the group, share and explain each of your stories for each loop. Design is driven by action and reflection in a certain direction. Share the rationale for your action.
- [ ] Together, find the stories/arguments which hold true and which fall short. Directed actions bind stories together. Write this down.

DAYS 33-39

LAST ROUND OF REFLECTION, STORYTELLING AND PROTO

INDIVIDUAL WORK

Aim
Reflect on what you have learned

Process
- [ ] Make reflections R#7, R#8, R#9, R#10, R#11.
- [ ] Take turns and share the reflections on first R#7, then R#8, etc.
- [ ] Note great points from others' reflections, and collectively make joint reflections.

TEAMWORK

Aim
Storytell the position.

Process
- [ ] With the previous work, you now have parts of the content for your design report in loops I, II, III and IV. Now you need to visualise and write it up for others to understand. Find context, detail and situation rich documentation, such as photos from user testing. Mark or note insights directæy on the images.
- [ ] Storytell what you did and what it leads to. Think of this as a client presentation. You want it to explain the significance and thoroughness of your research and design work, so clients have learnt the same as you when they have read your design report. The key is to lead them through your line of reasoning.
- [ ] As for your design, visualise and present it in time (e.g. a storyboard), in different contexts and situations, with a person (scale), about products on the market. Show us renders, expanded views, functional drawings, technical drawings, prototypes and user reactions.
- [ ] This part is about convincing us you identified the right problem and designed the right solution.

INSTRUCTION | Video 12: Prototyping for integration

TEAMWORK

Aim
Create illustrative/demonstrative prototypes

Process
- [ ] List all the key aspects your prototype needs to explain (e.g. size, colours, materials, folding mechanisms etc.
- [ ] Then consider and discuss how each aspect might best be illustrated. For instance, injection-moulded plastic or specially made metal pieces may be explained through 3D prints that are painted the right colour/texture and then supported with material samples.
- [ ] Difficult technologies or mechanical principles may be explained through other inspirational/aspirational products.
- [ ] Sizes and shapes need to be shown in full-scale models in foam, wood etc.
- [ ] The experiment may need to be rendered in 3D and placed in an environment.

THEORY IN BRIEF
DESIGNERLY METHODOLOGICAL APPROACHES

To become a designer, you need to learn to go through a design process, learn different methods and acquire certain hard and soft design skills. Nonetheless, during a master's programme in design, the biggest challenge is not to learn how to draw, do solid work, 3D print, prototype, involve users or go through the five-step process model of design thinking. We consider design education today to be quite skilled at conveying and training that—and we are not saying it is easy—it takes time, effort and dedication to learn such skills. However, we know there already are many resources and great material on these topics. (Incidentally, let's face it: Designers invent new processes and methods and learn new skills, materials and production processes continuously.)

While such skills belong to the design profession, they do not alone make you a competent, proficient or expert designer. To move up the skill acquisition ladder, the biggest challenge in becoming a design expert is to learn to see, act, learn and reflect as a designer, as opposed to a scientist, manager or another profession.

49 Laursen, L. N., & Haase, L. M. (2019). The shortcomings of design thinking when compared to designerly thinking. The Design Journal, 22(6), pp. 813–832.

DESIGN THINKING VS. DESIGNERLY THINKING

In our earlier research, we found that the main difference between 'design thinking'
(typically targeting people outside the design field, novices or professionals interested in doing a design) and 'designerly thinking' (targeting students within the design field whose priority is on acquiring a design skill and learning to design) is the focus and priorities of what they do and, hence, what they were taught. While both work with processes and tools and discuss the design paradigm, the central difference is 'designerly thinking'; the primary focus is the methodological approach. Methodological approaches are 'guidelines concerning how best to approach a given problem and how to competently select, configure, apply and evaluate the tools and techniques needed to tackle that problem'. [49]

Yes, we know that sounds a bit hairy and abstract in the particular academic theory of science kind of way. This notebook has been centred on learning, training and becoming aware of a distinctive designerly methodological approach. From the key literature concerning designerly thinking, we have identified six central methodological approaches that are significant to building design expertise. In our research of expert designers, we found that they are central to understanding what designers think and do—and the content and structure of this book is centred on modelling a doing approach, where you act to practice and internalise these methodological approaches. In this section, you will reflect on these six and what they mean.

REFLECTION #7 **DESIGNERLY METHODOLOGICAL APPROACHES**[50]

Modal shift

Rapid shifts between aspects of the task and modes of activity.

Designerly thinkers rapidly switch their attention between tasks and types of activities.[51] For instance, they might focus on the overall project and then on a smaller detail of the project, or they might rapidly shift between analysis, synthesis and evaluation. This modal shift has been found to heighten the quality of the eventual solution.[52]

As aspects, elements and factors in a design situation are measured along different scales and domains, there is no right perspective for seeing a problem or correct way of relating perspectives. Design is at its core about bringing together elements, perspectives and aspects. Design has no subject matter of its own; it synthesises and integrates various subject matters. In fact, this may be one of the most valuable abilities of design.[53]

On this page, please draw or note your reflection how you have done modal shifts. What is easy or challenging? How would you do it next time? Think about it regarding your other experiences and projects. Is it any different?

---

50 Laursen & Haase (2019). The shortcomings of design thinking when compared to designerly thinking. The Design Journal.
51 Akin, Ö., & Lin, C. (1995). Design protocol data and novel design decisions. Design Studies, 16(2), 211–236.
52 Cross, N. (2006). Design as a discipline. Designerly Ways of Knowing, 95–103.
53 Lawson, B. (2006). How designers think: The design process demystified. Routledge.

REFLECTION #8 **DESIGNERLY METHODOLOGICAL APPROACHES**[54]

Framing

Reflecting and challenging both the solution and problem through rephrasing.

During the process of reflective practice, the practitioner frames or reframes the design situation.[55] 'In design, a problem is never comprehensively stated. Design is as much about discovering the problem as it is about creating solutions'.[56] Framing serves as a working hypothesis or as a direction for the project, which is then tested. There is a lack of any boundary, field or knowledge that might be useful in a design project. There is no limit or boundary around the domains on which a design might draw.

Buchanan described framing as a source of new ideas and opportunities.[57] Reframing allows the rephrasing of the problem or the situation, which is thereby extended beyond the obvious to determine whether the problem is in fact a symptom of another problem and, eventually, to identify the core of both the problem and the solution.[58] 'At the core of design is the ability to work things out afresh to meet entirely new situations'.[59]

On this page, please draw or note your reflection on how you have framed the project or different parts of it. What is easy or challenging? Has it been clear? What have you learnt? How would you do it next time?

---

54 Laursen & Haase (2019). The shortcomings of design thinking when compared to designerly thinking. The Design Journal.
55 Schön, D. (1938). The reflective practitioner. New York, 1083.
56 Lawson, B. (2018). The design student's journey: Understanding how designers think. Routledge, p 72.
57 Buchanan, R. (1992). Wicked problems in design thinking. Design Issues, 8(2), 5–21.
58 Dorst, K. (2015). Frame innovation: Create new thinking by design. MIT Press.
59 Lawson, B. (2018). The design student's journey: Understanding how designers think. Routledge, p. 27.

REFLECTION #9 **DESIGNERLY METHODOLOGICAL APPROACHES**[60]

Co-development of the problem and solution.

Reflecting on and challenging both the solution and problem through rephrasing.

> Scientists and designers were given the same problem. While the scientist began by trying to analyse the problem, the designer began by trying to create solutions. Through the failings of their solutions, the designers tended to get a better understanding of the problem.[61]

In designerly thinking, this approach means that, rather than trying to first understand the problem and then to solve it (the standard process involved in most problem-solving methodologies), designers engage in an iterative process of suggesting and evaluating proposals. Meanwhile, a greater understanding of both the problem and the solution emerges.[62]

On this page, please draw or note your reflections on how you have coevolved a problem and solution space. How does this feel like not knowing either the problem or the solution? How do you know you are on the right track? What is easy or challenging? How would you do it next time? Think about your past semester projects. Is it any different?

---

[60] Laursen & Haase (2019). The shortcomings of design thinking when compared to designerly thinking. The Design Journal.
[61] Lawson, B. (2018). The design student's journey: Understanding how designers think. Routledge. p.
[62] Dorst, K., & Cross, N. (2001). Creativity in the design process: Co-evolution of problem–solution. Design Studies, 22(5), 425–437.

Reflections:

REFLECTION #10 **DESIGNERLY METHODOLOGICAL APPROACHES**[63]

Dialogue with the situation.

Visual and physical creations drive the process on more levels and between people.

Designers work through representations, drawings and models. The creation of models, sketches and prototypes is a key approach for capturing the tacit knowledge relevant to the design situation and transforming it into testable proposals or solutions.[64] Rather than gradual refinement, radical changes can be envisioned in such a process. 'Design by drawing' gives the designer a 'greater perceptual span'.[65]

Drawings of ideas and concepts hold aspirations that challenge the making process in design. In this regard, the creation of physical artefacts becomes a central aspect of making 'intuitive knowing in the midst of action' apparent (reflection in action) as well as a means of making decisions about the next step (reflection on action).[66]

On this page, please draw or note your reflection on your considerations of having a dialogue with the situation. What happens when you draw? Model? Create proposals? Was it difficult? Easy? Did it change along the way? What advice would you give yourself for the next time? How would you do it differently?

---

[63] Laursen & Haase (2019). The shortcomings of design thinking when compared to designerly thinking, The Design Journal.
[64] Cross, N. (2006). Design as a discipline. Designerly Ways of Knowing, 95–103.
[65] Jones, J. C. (1966). Design methods reviewed. In The Design Method (pp. 295–309). Springer, Boston, MA.
[66] Schön, D. (1938). The reflective practitioner. New York, 1083.

REFLECTION #11 **DESIGNERLY METHODOLOGICAL APPROACHES**[67]

Solution-led goal analysis.

Focus on creating the right solution rather than qualifying the goal.

Designers work in a solution-focused manner. They are more interested in creating designs than in understanding the problem. They focus on identifying the right solution[68] and ensuring that the identified solution is meaningful to both the users and the context.[69] This approach involves searching for a deeper understanding of users' aspirational values and priorities as well as identifying a path towards the most desirable future.[70] Thus, design is prescriptive, in a sense. Instead of analysing, describing or navigating the existing world, design suggests how the world might be.[71]

Such a solution-focused approach, however, presents a pitfall. At some point in the process, designers typically become too attached to a specific design idea. The proposal that helped the designer understand the problem becomes a blocker of progress. Sometimes, they become so attached to it that it feels like they must restart their project when they have to reframe the concept to a new line of thought. Thus, the goal needs to be subject to changes along the way.[72]

On this page, please draw or note your reflections on whether you have made a solution-led goal analysis (that is, developed a solution and figured out whether it represented the right goal). How has your goal changed during your process? When was it easy or difficult for you? Why? How would you approach or handle this next time?

---

[67] Laursen and Haase (2019). The shortcomings of design thinking when compared to designerly thinking. The Design Journal.
[68] Cross, N. (2006). Design as a discipline. Designerly Ways of Knowing, 95–103.
[69] Krippendorff, K. (2005). The semantic turn: A new foundation for design. CRC Press.
[70] Dorst, K. (2011). The core of 'design thinking' and its application. Design Studies, 32(6), 521–532.
[71] Lawson, B. (2006). How designers think: The design process demystified. Routledge.
[72] Cross, N. (2006). Design as a discipline. Designerly Ways of Knowing, 95–103.

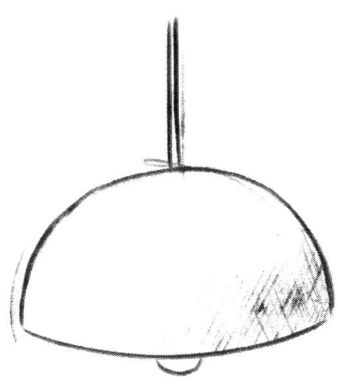
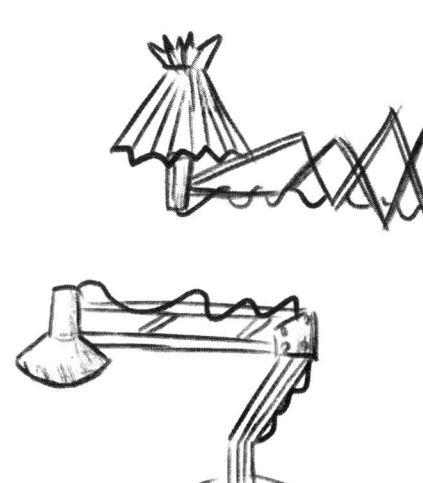

REFLECTION #12 **DESIGNERLY METHODOLOGICAL APPROACHES**[73]

REFLECTIVE PRACTICE.

Reflection in action and reflection on action (process reflection).

In particular, the extensive work of Schön[74] and, later, the work of Lawson,[75] Cross[76] and Buchanan[77] have pointed to reflective practice as a widely used approach to designerly thinking, since it allows competent practitioners to utilise their tacit knowledge through a 'conversation' with the situation, during which they shift between reflection in action (while doing) and reflection on action (process reflection).

Reflect on your reflection...

---

[73] Laursen & Haase (2019). The shortcomings of design thinking when compared to designerly thinking. The Design Journal.
[74] Schon, D. (1938). The reflective practitioner. New York, 1083.
[75] Lawson, B. (2006). How designers think: The design process demystified. Routledge.
[76] Cross, N. (2006). Design as a discipline. Designerly Ways of Knowing, 95–103.
[77] Buchanan, R. (1992). Wicked problems in design thinking. Design Issues, 8(2), 5–21.